# HOW TO TEACH AN OLD DOG NEW TRICKS

## Retraining the Secondhand Dog

## Books by Kurt Unkelbach

How to Teach an Old Dog New Tricks
   *Retraining the Secondhand Dog*
Uncle Charlie's Poodle
How to Make Money in Dogs
How to Bring Up Your Pet Dog
Love on a Leash
Those Lovable Retrievers
Murphy
Albert Payson Terhune: The Master of Sunnybank
The Winning of Westminster
The Pleasures of Dog Ownership (*with his wife*)
The Dog in My Life
The Dog Who Never Knew
Ruffian: International Champion
Winning Ways
Both Ends of the Leash
You're a Good Dog, Joe
A Cat and His Dogs
Catnip
Tiger Up a Tree
The American Dog Book
How to Show Your Dog and Win
Best of Breeds Guide for Young Dog Lovers

# HOW TO TEACH AN

Kurt Unkelbach
*Illustrated by Sam Savitt*

# OLD DOG NEW TRICKS

## Retraining the Secondhand Dog

DODD, MEAD & COMPANY
New York

To Rosemary

Library of Congress Cataloging in Publication Data

Unkelbach, Kurt.
  How to teach an old dog new tricks.

  Includes index.
  SUMMARY: A guide to retraining dogs once owned by
other masters.
  1. Dogs—Training. [1. Dogs—Training] I. Savitt,
Sam. II. Title.
SF431.U54      636.7'08'8      78-22430
ISBN 0-396-07669-6

# CONTENTS

# ON THESE PAGES . . .

While this guide is designed primarily for second owners who cannot live contentedly with their new dogs, the advice is also appropriate for first, third, and fourth owners of pups or adult canines that persist in doing unappreciated or socially improper things.

Unless corrected, the dog that is permitted to run the show in whole or in part will destroy any chance of a satisfying owner-pet relationship. The longer you wait, the more difficult the task, since bad habits become ingrained and your lovable beast lacks both the intelligence and the ambition to reform himself.

These pages will tell you how to retrain your dog to suit your desires while limiting his or her capability to train you. The tested-and-proven advice is based on experience. It has worked for us and for our friends and it should work for you.

May the tail wagger in your life really deserve your effort, companionship, and love.

K.U.

# HOW TO TEACH AN OLD DOG NEW TRICKS

## Retraining the Secondhand Dog

*Chapter 1*

# THE SECOND TIME AROUND

While most animal lovers know that the dog is man's best friend, quite a few dogs are either blissfully unaware of this fact or couldn't care less, and a surprising number of these dogs are now residing in their second permanent home or will be tomorrow. If you are the current owner of such a dog, you are probably wondering why he isn't living up to his reputation as a delight to have around the house, or how such a "completely" trained pet can make such a shambles of your nervous system and peaceful life.

The *easy* solution is to find another, third, owner for the dog, but very few people adopt this ploy. The biggest reason for this is family relations. According to pet industry statistics, there are now more than forty million pet dogs in the United States, and an overwhelming majority of transfers of ownership—aside from direct sales—can be attributed to the inheritance factor. In this nation of dog lovers, it is simply unthinkable to send Brutus to a dog pound when Uncle Harry moves to a nursing home. And consider cute Sweetypie, the adorable Lhasa Apso who filled the lonely hours of beloved, wealthy, and now late Aunt Lizzie, who remembered both of you in her will.

In recent history, more than a million dogs per annum have changed hands between relatives because the original owner has moved or died or found it impossible to continue providing care. That figure is sure to be repeated this year. To reach a grand total of new second owners per annum, add the array of those who take over from friends, friends of friends, and sometimes strangers. The latter have lost their dogs—by accident or design—and those homeless dogs find new owners on their own or through animal shelters.

Whatever the source or the means of acquiring a dog once owned by somebody else, all of the dogs—the well trained and the barely trained—will need some amount of *re*training to fit into the lifestyles of their new owners and keep them reasonably happy. The exceptional pet canine, the one who pleases his second owner as much as his first, is as rare as an August blizzard in Miami. Happily, the dog who can't be

retrained is almost as rare, although he or she has no way of getting this point across to a new master. The average second owner, aware that the canine is also a social animal, frequently overestimates his new pet's intelligence and really expects the dog to correct himself in due time—perhaps with a little polite reminding.

It doesn't happen that way. A dog must be taught to do things *your* way, and the teaching is necessarily more time consuming if your way contradicts the former owner's golden rule. The dog that corrects a sin without guidance does so by accident and will probably revert to form before the cheering stops. He isn't trying to be a bad dog, but he's not capable of reasoning at our level and it's up to us to impose our will—or start climbing walls. He won't reform himself.

Whatever the pet dog's sex, age, breed or nonbreed,

canine capability for retrainability is always present, granted the animal is normal in certain respects. Normality means that the dog is friendly (as opposed to vicious or terribly shy), healthy, and not hampered by blindness, deafness, or a crippling deformity. Any normal dog, then, is capable of learning new things—and forgetting old habits, for that matter. How much or how little he learns is the mystery, and it's always dependent on the master's talent as a teacher.

Whenever skeptics push me into a corner and demand an example of a normal dog that made good in a dramatically different environment, I refer to the case of a dog named Toby. He was a big and gentle Labrador, friendly with everybody, beautifully behaved, and as close as a dog can come to being a perfect house pet. He belonged to my wife, and she loaned him to the Army's K-9 Corps during World War II, and there he was retrained into a sentry dog, loyal to only one man. He served overseas and at war's end went through a rehabilitation course to prepare him for his return to family life. When Toby came home, he was his old self again, and he never gave Evie or me or anyone else any trouble. Thousands of other dogs went through the same routines, and I can't recall hearing of a single one preferring war to peace. So if your dog is being difficult, have faith.

Dogs are not like peas in a pod, of course, and some are more cooperative, some more obstinate, than others. Still, the dog game's veterans manage to agree on a few generalities: females are more amenable and thus easier to retrain, pups cooperate at a faster clip than adults, and a beautiful purebred is not necessarily brighter than an unkempt mutt of mixed parentage. As for the pure breeds, sporting dogs are the most agreeable, terriers are the stubbornest, and

hounds the slowest at turning over a new leaf. Working and non-sporting dogs are about average in retrainability, but there's no rating on the toys, those little dogs designed for spoiling and closet-size apartments. Please keep in mind that the generalities are not guarantees, since there are oafs in every breed, including the multitudinous mixed breeds.

If you are on the verge of becoming the second owner of a purebred and have a choice of breeds, and not much faith in generalities, it won't do you any harm to consider this seldom printed truth: unless you are endowed with a wisdom surpassing that of any genuine canine authority, gift dogs belonging to the most popular breeds arrive completely equipped with the biggest potential for trouble. This is the fault of some of the breeders, not the dogs.

As the night follows the day, the more popular the breed, the more the demand for pups, and, to meet that demand, the greater the number of breeders specializing in that breed. And as another day follows the night, the percentage of dingbat breeders—those who don't know what they're doing and don't care, but hope to make money at it—is always higher in the twenty most popular breeds. Those dingbat breeders are responsible for most of the poor-quality purebred pups, the ones that are the most difficult to train or retrain. And those same pups are the most likely to carry inherited defects that often amount to both heavy expense and heartbreak.

All other things being equal, if you don't know much about a dog's breeding or breeder, a Labrador Retriever (my breed) is a much poorer bet than a Flat-Coated Retriever, and an Irish Setter is a bigger risk than a Gordon Setter, and a Yorkshire Terrier will be a bigger headache than a Sealyham Terrier.

Whether you are about to become a certain dog's second owner or are already in possession, you will be retraining in the dark if your knowledge about the former owner is limited. If that person was excitable, the new pup or dog in your life may be close to a nervous wreck and will require a settling-in period of several weeks before he trusts you enough to learn from you. If the person was a perfectionist —particularly when it comes to obedience—it may take even longer for the dog to sense that your heart is in the right place. And if the first owner was the indulgent type and thought that the dog would somehow train himself sooner or later, then the sooner the better for the start of your retraining program, although you must expect early resistance from any new pet.

A dog will not adapt to your home and ways as rapidly as a cat, and a major reason why is the canine's inability to take a sudden change of environment in stride. Such a change is a very emotional experience and much more difficult for him to accept than it is for us to move into a new home, or change towns, schools, or jobs. Whereas we can anticipate and prepare, a complete change for him comes as both a surprise and a shock.

Whatever the dog's age, sex, temperament, and background, it will take anywhere from some time to a long time for him to settle into his new situation and realize that he has nothing to fear from the strange people, scents, sounds, walls, rugs and furniture. If you think that's overemphasizing your new dog's anxieties, remember that you have only changed from nonowner to owner, whereas he has changed worlds.

Until the trauma of the transitional period fades away, training will not be effective and judgments about the dog's behavior and learning ability should be put in abeyance. Plenty of human companionship is a must and keeping him at home helps. Taking him on a tour of the neighborhood and introducing him to all acquaintances simply enlarges the new, strange world and prolongs his uneasiness.

The older the dog, the longer it will take him or her to adjust. By that established rule of canine life, pups are very open to suggestion, and pet-shop pups offer amazing proof. Weaned too early (4 weeks), the pups are shipped to a wholesaler (5 weeks) who places them with pet shops (6 weeks) where they are sold (at 7 and 8 weeks) to gullible dog lovers. That's four changes (sometimes more) of environment in just a few weeks and, considering deplorable travel, housing, and care, it's a wonder that any of the baby canines survive. Still, enough do to illustrate the amazing adaptability of young pups under conditions that are outlawed in a few states but not always enforced.

This is a simple way to lessen the emotional impact for the dog changing homes. It shortens the transitional period and makes it possible for the new owner to begin any needed training at an earlier date. This method involves a little planning and cooperation between owners (original and second, or breeder and puppy buyer) and consists of alternate choices:

*Plan A*

This is the best method. The original owner takes Rover on a visit to the home of his owner-to-be. Rover meets the members of his next family and is allowed to roam about the residence at will. Nobody makes a fuss over him, but he is petted when he seems to want attention. If the visit can be timed to include his daily meal, fine and dandy. The visit should last for at least an hour.

Now Rover has experienced the sights, sounds, and smells of his next permanent world. The transfer, when it comes, will not throw him for a total loss.

The more those social visits occur, the more easily Rover will adapt to the permanent change and the happier his new owner will be. Six visits over a two-week period would make this a better than best method, or ideal. Rover would probably be anxious to please and learn something new on his third or fourth day after the move.

## Plan B

This is the next best method and can be adopted when it is impossible or too inconvenient for the original owner to accompany Rover on Plan A visits. Before assuming ownership, the new master pays several visits to Rover's current home so that he and the dog can establish some rapport. Finally, something Rover likes should go with him to his new home. His favorite toy or well-chewed nylon bone, or perhaps the pillow or throw rug that has been his bed. Even dogs need security blankets.

If you are about to become Rover's new owner and disregard both plans, you'll just have to live with his bad habits for a longer period than is really necessary. Second owners of inherited dogs are sometimes at a disadvantage, of course, since the first owners (the people who wrote the wills) are no longer around to cooperate. Still, it's always possible to bring home some kind of security blanket and it will always help.

The effectiveness of either plan depends on the presence of the new owner. All groundwork, preparations, and the warm welcome become wasted efforts if the dog panics, and he's pretty sure to do so if he is left alone for an extended period of time (a couple of hours) during the first few days. This doesn't mean that the new dog must sit on your lap night and day, but he should know that you're around and that he's not deserted. Any degree of panic can result in the destruction of worthwhile objects and the complete loss of good manners, and also set back the time for training to begin. If you plan on introducing Rover to your home on Saturday morning but you intend to have dinner out and then go to a movie, delay the dog's arrival until Sunday. Sorry about the inconvenience.

The big idea, of course, is to put the new dog at ease before lowering the retraining boom. And it's a fine time to prove to the world that you are extremely wise for your years and far more considerate than the average dog lover, whose concern for canine health is confined to whenever his pet becomes ill. This is strange, for good health and canine aptitude go hand in hand. Love for one's dog is nice but not enough.

You should see to it that your dog gets enough daily exercise (a matter of experiment) and stays close to his proper weight. Your dog is at the right weight for him (although not necessarily for his breed) when he is lean, a compromise between fat and skinny. When lean, his ribs do not protrude but you have no trouble finding them with your fingers. One must always use the touch system to check out a dog with a long or shaggy coat, of course.

It's always best for the dog when he's at proper weight, but his pounds come from the food he's fed, and an amazing number of commercial dog foods do not come close to any canine's nutritional requirements. In the crazy world of dog foods and free-spending dog lovers, the widely promoted and most expensive brands aren't always the wisest choices. While all the brands can be assumed to have sufficient amounts of carbohydrates, vitamins, and minerals, a great many are sorely deficient in those other important essentials, protein and fat. Of course the canine also requires water, but why buy it?

The popular brand foods are known as dry (kibble, meal) and wet (canned). Whether dry or wet, the label carries an analysis of contents in percentages. An adult canine needs a minimum of 20 percent protein, while a growing pup requires 25 percent, and 6 to 7 percent fat is right for both. A label also carries a listing of ingredients in order of quantity, and a good brand has one or more of these among the first three: meat, bonemeal, and meat by-products. There's nothing wrong with vegetable protein, but animal protein is easier for a dog to digest.

It is reasonable to assume that anyone who can read small print, with or without a magnifying glass, should be able to keep his dog on a sufficiently nutritious diet, but that is not the case. In this country and everywhere else, a majority of pet dogs exist on inadequate diets, mostly because their adoring owners do not understand that the prices and advertised promises of brands have no bearing on quality, or that a good wet brand is never as economical as a good dry brand. This is true because the wets contain at least 75 percent moisture, better known as water, which is far cheaper when it comes from the home tap.

Wet food needs no preparation and is served as it comes from the can. While dry food can be fed right from the container too, it is more palatable to the dog and easier to digest if it's moistened before serving. Kibble is more popular than meal with both owners and dogs, and you won't find any argument around here. The moistening amounts to soaking the kibble in water for ten or fifteen minutes. Just enough so that the soaked nuggets give a bit when pinched, but not so much that the nuggets are reduced to soup.

Like other veterans in the dog game, we are not content to feed kibble as it comes from the bag, even when soaked. All commercial dog foods are wildly promoted as being *balanced*, in the sense that the nutritional content is up to government standards. While the announced ingredients seem to warrant the claim, only a single brand bothers with government inspection. That particular food is usually unavailable in our home territory, so we feed one of the other ten thousand brands and add available odds and ends. For example, here's Evie's daily recipe for David, an eighty pounder:

Place six cups of kibble in dinner dish. Add two tablespoons of canned dog food, or similar amount of meat (raw or cooked, but always cooked pork), fowl, or fish left over from family meals. Add tablespoon of fat left over from family meals, or of suet. Add small amount of saved liquids (small quantities of soup, water vegetables were cooked in, gravy from previous meal, et cetera). Add sufficient water, if needed. Mix *well*, let stand for fifteen minutes, and serve.

Since David is just one of several Labs around here, it should be obvious that very little food fit for human consumption is wasted, and that the canine menu varies from day to day. And every day the dogs get more than any brand offers in protein, vitamins, and minerals.

While it is always wise to continue with a pet's customary diet in the beginning, keeping him on Brand ZZ forever is ridiculous if it doesn't meet the protein and fat requirements. Forget the first owner's advice, find and buy a proper brand, and make the switch—but do it gradually. The penalty for switching the dog from Brand ZZ to Brand OK in too much of a hurry is always diarrhea. While the quantity of the meal remains constant, the new brand should be introduced at a rate of no more than 20 percent per day. If diarrhea then occurs, call a halt to the exchange, add a hardboiled egg to meals for a few days (or substitute boiled rice for half of his usual food), then proceed at a cautious 10 percent per day clip.

In his new environment (yours), the pup or dog may display utter contempt for whatever food you offer him. He's either a finicky eater, stubborn, or confused, and how to handle him will be explained on the pages to follow. For now, it is sufficient to realize that you know what's good for

*"Please, Tiger . . ."*

your dog. He doesn't, and chances are that his first owner didn't.

Ah, that first owner. If you are still taking advice from him (her), you are probably barking up the wrong tree. You wouldn't be retraining the pooch now if the original owner had done the right things, so seeking that person's advice after the day of transfer can't help very much, if at all. Still, if you must ask him for advice, do it over the phone or in a letter. Inviting him to drop in for a visit is sure to hurt your retraining cause. At all costs, keep your dog's first master away from him as long as possible—if not forever, for at least a year. Respecting, loving, and obeying one master at a time is quite enough for any dog, especially at retraining time. He doesn't need confusion.

*Chapter 2*

# THE GENTLE ART OF CONNING

Just about every other secondhand dog in the land arrives in his new home as a gift. And something of a surprise, in the sense that the new owner had no idea last week that he would be responsible for the welfare of a dog this week. There's nothing legally or morally wrong with that, of course, and both pet and owner would live in happy harmony if every dog lover was born with the talent to teach canines. Since that is not the case, common sense dictates that anyone incapable of teaching a dog should not own one, unless he enjoys feeling trapped in an awkward situation. If you do not have the potential for bending a dog to your will, it is wiser and far less troublesome to own such other pets as canaries, tropical fish, and hamsters.

Psychologists, animal behaviorists, and other deep thinkers agree that a person who can't get along with a child will have a heck of a time with dogs. They vacillate about the precise age of the child, but anyone who has observed dogs and their lovers for more than a score of years will agree that if you can't handle a six-year-old child, your chances of training a dog are close to nil. Using methods that are socially acceptable, that is. By beating the daylights out of a little child or a dog, it is possible to train either one to stay off a new sofa. However, that's fear training, a method with many variations, none of them approved by genuine dog lovers, sane parents, nice children, and this book.

Now we know why Alice, aged eleven and often in complete charge of her younger brother Billy for hours at a time, had no real trouble retraining Rudolph, the oversized St. Bernard gift from Uncle Ted, who had named the dog Holy Terror. "Either the dog goes or I move," Aunt Pansy had threatened. "Why don't you give the big bum to Alice? She can get that brat Billy to do almost anything."

While Alice is not considered precocious by those who know her, she has already grasped a fundamental that is not understood by the average dog lover: we tend to overrate any dog's intelligence, misinterpret instinct for brilliance, and often accuse him of stubbornness when he really doesn't understand. Normally, any child of six is much smarter than an adult dog, and the latter's intellect will not continue to develop. Yet most of us are child-indulgent and dog-impatient. Whilst training any dog, 'tis best to consider him as a very small and not very bright child.

Since you are reading this page, you have to be far more

intelligent than any dog on record. If you are able to control a small child, then you can teach your dog to do something new or restrain him from doing something undesirable. So long as that something isn't ridiculous and perfection is not demanded, there's no reason why you can't train your dog to do things your way. Because of your superior intellect, you have all the advantages, whereas all your dog has going for him is the desire to be doing something else, and that's never impossible to overcome.

Half the battle (but not the war) is won if you can accept conning as a superior substitute for training. The concept puts fun into teaching and makes it less of a task for you, less of a bore and irritant for the dog. The pet ends up doing something your way without really knowing it. As they say in Bamboo, he has been bamboozled.

To con or bamboozle properly, a little advance thinking is required. Although overlooked in standard lectures on training, these fundamentals of conning are worth contemplating:

## THE RIGHT MOOD

You cannot be an effective con artist if you are angry, irritated, nervous, worried, ill, weary, bored, or pressed for time. The individual dog will learn at his own speed, and time is wasted when you are not in the right frame of mind. 'Tis better to skip a training session than confuse a canine student by not being your true, considerate, wonderful self.

## A WINNING VOICE

Compared to man's sense of hearing, the canine's is acute, and he can hear better with one ear than we can with a pair. Thus, your normal vocal volume—the one you employ when chatting with a friend in a small room, average elevator, or compact car—is correct.

Achieving the proper tone of voice is another matter and sometimes a bit difficult. A good con artist uses a pleasant tone that's garnished with a touch of firmness. The idea is to let the dog know that you are his friend, but that you still mean business.

Tone is so important that you can consider yours still inadequate if the dog fails to respond in the early stages of training. For those who run into difficulty, achieving the right tone is a matter of practice, and long, solitary walks in the forest or a park are recommended. Command trees to stand, bushes to sit, rocks to stay.

Baby talk is sweet, not really pleasant, and unproductive. Avoid using it in training. If you find refraining impossible, avoid becoming the second owner of a dog. Whenever you observe an owner using baby talk to get his dog to do something, you can be pretty sure the tables have been turned: the dog is the con artist and has tricked the owner into acting like an idiot.

## THE TIME TO TRAIN

Any time is the right time for training, so long as you are in the right mood. The dog won't care whether it's morning or afternoon, sunny or raining, Monday or Friday. As for the wisdom of training before or after the dog's daily meal, it's a question of whom to believe. Veteran trainers are divided about equally, so toss a coin or suit your own convenience. However, if you join the before school-of-thought and you feed your dog on schedule—about the same time every day—the thirty minutes preceding this important event in his day amount to an unreceptive period. A healthy dog will have food on his mind and won't really concentrate on anything else.

Otherwise, your own common sense will tell you when to train. The time is only important when the training amounts to correcting, or retraining, as when the dog consistently does something that is illegal in your home. You have no choice when a canine infraction of house rules occurs: dashing through doorway, chewing chair leg, ripping pillow, wetting rug, emptying wastebasket. Correction is immediate and on the spot. Let's say that your pet dashes ahead of you when you open a door. The first owner didn't mind, but you do. For best results, the correction should be prompt, and then repeated as often as necessary. If you wait even ten seconds and say, "That wasn't very polite of you, Lassie. Next time, please follow me," the dog will only be puzzled. The canine doesn't remember much, and he's not concerned with the meaning of words. He will recall an act (your physical correction) and related sounds (your simultaneous command words) if both are repeated whenever he sins. If you are persistent, he will learn to cooperate and not dash through the doorway ahead of you and knock over everything in his way.

## THE TRAINING SITE

For general training, such as teaching a dog to sit or come, the conditions are far more important than the place. Indoors or outdoors, the fewer the distractions the better. If you can't hold the dog's attention, you might as well try to teach a can of tuna fish to bark. Achieving any kind of rapport with your pet is just about impossible in front of an audience. The advice, comments, questions, and giggles from friends, loved ones, and curious onlookers never prove helpful.

Weather permitting, I prefer to train outdoors and believe that my dogs appreciate sunshine and fresh air as much as I do. Finding a site away from other people is no problem where I live, but I cannot control butterflies, flights of honking wild geese, shouts and other noises from afar that I cannot hear, and tempting scents that ride the breezes. Still, I can always invent some distraction to blame on a day when my conning fails to work.

### The Attention Span of *Canis Familiaris*

A dog's love for his master cannot be measured by how long he stays interested in learning something. Pups lose interest in a hurry, and that's why very short training sessions are advised, although several sessions can and should be held per day. If you can con a young pup into thinking that he's having fun, the chances of keeping him interested are better, and he'll go for as long as five minutes before becoming bored. Not stubborn, but bored.

That being true, it's reasonable to assume that an adult dog will concentrate on a lesson for twenty-five minutes or a little more. That is a popular belief, it has been proven by countless researchers, I don't know an authority who disputes it—and it makes me wonder if I have been living in a dream world. I agree with the young pup's attention span and also find it amazing when compared to a human baby's, but there's something cockeyed about the adult dog's figures. Twenty-five minutes of concentration is certainly not the norm for the majority of the dogs I've owned, known, and observed in various stages of training. The average adult canine will concentrate—or whatever a dog does that we call concentration—for ten to fifteen minutes per session.

When it comes to learning and performing, Obedience dogs are the professionals of the canine world. They are constantly in training during their careers, and that day is unusual when they are not learning something new or perfecting something they already have down pat. If you are not familiar with the sport of Obedience (see Chapter 7), attend a trial and observe well-trained dogs (mostly adults) in action. Here, it is only important to know that there are exercises in the Open class when all the dogs in that class (fifteen usually) sit and lie. For the Long Sit, the dogs sit in line for three minutes, and for the Long Down, it's five minutes. The handlers of the dogs are not present for the durations, nor are they within view of the dogs. To succeed and garner points, each dog must sit and then lie on the ground, motionless or almost so, for the specified periods of time.

These well-trained dogs have been through the exercises many times before, and they are as immune as an animal can be to such distractions as crowds, noises, strange scents, and their peers. Each dog knows what's expected of him, so sitting or relaxing on the ground for a few minutes is certainly not a big deal. Wouldn't you think that every dog present would pass the tests with flying colors? It seldom happens. Usually, one dog will forget all his training and take a stroll. That's enough to break the concentration of others. At the trial, all the offenders are losers. Back home, they're sure to get stiff refresher courses from their masters.

I have continued at length on this subject for good reason: to reassure any second owner that everybody has a certain amount of trouble training dogs, and if you think your new pet is impossible, there are thousands of second owners who would tell you that you are having an easy time by comparison. Maybe you've been trying too much too often, and for too long. Measure your dog's attention span by trial and error, then fit the general training into those minutes.

*"My dear Hootowl Pete ..."*

LOUDER THAN WORDS

A great many dogs look as if they understand every word that's spoken to them, so it's only natural that their owners feel that they are dealing with wise pets. And that's why so many people feel discouraged when training dogs. The ungrateful beasts don't realize they are being trained, and are so uncooperative that their handlers have a hard time controlling tempers.

Take the case of Hootowl Pete. Since his first owner was haphazard about training, the dog didn't learn much beyond eating food and rugs, digging holes in the lawn, and playing in mud holes after a rainstorm. Pete's second owner decided to reform him, and she set aside thirty minutes every day for training. Every day at five—as soon as she returned home from school—she would hold Pete's head in her hand, look him in the eyes, and say, "My dear Hootowl Pete, it is now five o'clock sharp, time once again for a half hour of training. Please, just this once, try to pay attention." Pete never did understand what she was saying, and today he is driving his third owner batty.

Appealing to a dog's better nature is not the way to prepare him for a training session. The trick is in his collar—or collars, if you prefer. The one he wears every day as a matter of course, and his training collar. The latter speaks louder than words. When you remove his pet collar and replace it with his training collar, the dog—after a few such experiences—knows that the moment of truth has arrived and another learning period is about to begin.

There are several kinds of training collars on the market, but the only one recommended here is the simplest and kindest (to the dog) of all. It's a slip collar, nylon or chain. Around here we use the nylon for every day, the chain for training. More about collars in the next chapter.

## The Importance of Socialization

It will probably not come as news that the domestic canine is a social animal, in that he is a firm believer in family life and is rarely a loner. Fortunately for us, he is quite willing to accept people as members of his family and is happy when we return the favor. It's entirely possible that he regards us as oddball canines who went wrong. We must seem like a strange, upright pack to him.

Whatever his opinion of us, we know more about him than he ever will and are free to use this knowledge to our advantage. For example, and there are no two ways about this, a dog that is constantly in the company of people makes a vastly superior pet to the dog that lives in a kennel and sees people daily, but not for hours at a time. The only exception would be a dog living with cruel people.

Most of us who deliberately spend as much time with dogs as with people are great believers in socialization, a matter of helping a dog adjust to civilization in general. Once settled in, the new dog is taken to different places where he'll come into contact with strangers, hear new and sometimes ominous noises (factory whistles, sirens), experience scents not found at home, and see a variety of other animals and mobile things that are foreign to his daily routine. He must always be on leash during such adventures, of

*Socialization is important.*

course, and your role is to be reassuring when he demonstrates the slightest confusion or shyness. The overall objective is to mold a well-balanced dog, or at least better balanced than he would be if always left at home. A dog that has seen, heard, and smelled the world outside his four walls will not dive under the bed when lightning crashes and thunder rolls—unless his owner dives first and sets an example.

Now, just to cover every base, a dog wearing a collar and leash touring the town while sitting in a car is not adjusting to man's world, not even when his owner takes the trouble to explain, "That crowd is going into a supermarket; a man riding a motorcycle is directly ahead; in the field to your right are a cow and a horse, not related; we are now approaching the gasoline station owned by my cousin; and that waterfall on the billboard over there is not real." Well, maybe the dog is adjusting to the seat, but nothing more.

If your time is limited or you lack the confidence to handle socialization on your own, attending school with your dog might be the answer. Not just any old school, but an obedience school, where you'll learn how to handle your dog and he'll become accustomed to getting along with other people and strange dogs. See Chapter 7 for more about these schools.

# Chapter 3

# BASIC TOOLS AND TRAINING

COLLAR AND LEASH

Anyone who has owned a dog for more than a few hours knows that a collar and a leash are indispensable training tools. Still, most owners are not aware that the most practical combination of collar and leash is also the simplest and least expensive.

The three commonest types of dog collars are best known as the strap, the slip, and the martingale choke. A fourth type, often advertised as the professional trainer's choice (spiked or electric shock), is unfortunate, not used by any of the professionals I know, and does not rate further mention. As for the others:

*Strap.* Round or flat, this is a fixed collar that wraps around the dog's neck. Since it must be worn reasonably tight, there's no give and it's impractical for training. Usually made of leather, this is really a fashion item and it has these negative features: since dog can't escape collar, it can hang or choke him by catching on something; if wet, it will stay wet for hours, and might stain the coat; on smooth- and short-coated dogs, skin rash or eczema can result (beware the flea collar); and neck hairs on coated dogs will be

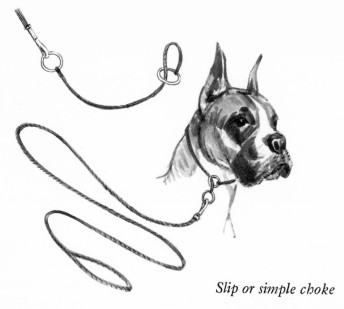

*Slip or simple choke*

broken. Wetness does not apply when the collar is made of chain, of course.

*Slip.* Also known as a simple choke, this amounts to a length of cord or light chain with a small metal ring at each end. The length is pushed through one ring to create a loop, or collar. When the leash is attached to the other ring (see illustration), a slight tug tightens the collar, making it ideal for training. The right size fits over the dog's head and hangs a little loose around the neck.

The nylon cord comes in a choice of colors, is washable, and won't break coat hairs. As reported earlier, here we use the nylon for a dog's everyday wear, and the light chain for training only. When a dog is not being supervised, nylon is safest. If the collar catches on something, the dog will either work the collar off or bite through it if he must.

The nylon collar is also the most economical one around. It usually costs only a few dollars, and that's much less than a quality strap collar. The small expense also helps at replacement time, when the collar no longer fits, is frayed, or lost.

The nylon slip is practical for most breeds, the exceptions being such long-coated canines as Samoyeds, Pulik, and Keeshonden, whose neck hairs tend to cling to nylon and clog the rings. Then the collar cannot work effectively and will break hairs. For such breeds, a better choice is the slip collar made of rounded leather. More expensive than the nylon, but longer lasting.

*Martingale choke.* Used for training the dog that is a little too strong or unruly for his handler. When a tug on the leash tightens the collar, the pressure is applied evenly around the dog's neck, he's easier to control, and he is not apt to choke. When you find it impossible to handle a dog on a slip collar, go to the martingale. Cord, leather, or chain, it costs more than a slip, but much less than a fancy strap. As for right size, the lower loop extended to maximum (see illustration)

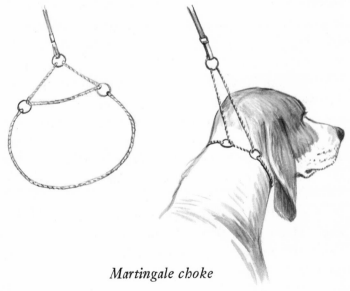

*Martingale choke*

should just fit over the dog's head and ears and hang a little loosely at the neck.

As for leashes, they come in a variety of styles, colors, and materials, and most aren't worth their price tags. They are impractical for a walk in the park or a training session, too easy to chew and destroy (unless made of chain), and usually too strong for the pets they are supposed to restrain. For some strange reason, and more so in America than elsewhere in the world, the average dog wears a collar needlessly strong and heavy and a burden to him, and the leash attached to it could be used to tow an elephant on wheels.

For everyday use and training, the canvas-web type is the choice of veterans in the dog game. While not as fashionable as the leather and chain leashes, it is lighter, durable enough, comes in a handy length (six feet), and still costs about four dollars. However, it is chewable, and a determined pup can slice his way through the half-inch width in about thirty minutes. While it is often safe to leave it with a pup, hanging it out of his reach is safer.

Some people don't believe in dog collars, and there's nothing wrong with that if a dog lives indoors most of the time and plays outdoors in a confined area. The trouble comes when the dog moves to his second home and the new owner, a bow-tie man—even in the shower—insists that the newcomer wear something around his neck, too. Nine times out of ten, the dog will act as if the strange thing is an enemy and go to war. He'll spend days trying to scratch it off, rub it off, and work it between his jaws for destruction. Whines, groans, and sleepless nights are a part of the resentment routine, and hunger strikes are common. In the long run, the dog will accept his fate. Meanwhile, until he does, training him to do anything else will be difficult and sometimes impossible.

*40*

But it doesn't have to be a long run. The successful introduction of a pup or adult to his collar amounts to no more than easy stages and a little conning. Three or four times a day, let him wear the collar for about five minutes. Stay close and distract him with small talk, petting, and playing. In a few days, he won't mind wearing the collar all the time, if that's what you want.

Once a dog accepts his collar as a harmless adornment, he's ready for the leash. Adults either accept it immediately or resent it and fight. With the fighters and pups, the simple solution to acceptance is the easy-stages conning theory. On the first day, attach the leash to the collar and permit the canine student to drag it around for a few minutes. Again, stay on the scene and practice conning. Repeat several times before going to bed. On the second day, the action is just the same for the first couple of sessions. After that, pick up the other end of the leash and let the student take you for a walk, preferably outdoors. He is the leader, you are the follower. It's all right for him to pull you, but try not to pull him, and avoid strong, sudden jerks. The more fun this is for the dog (or pup), the less he'll resent the leash, and the readier he is for simple, basic training.

## Basic Commands

There's not much sense owning a dog if the relationship is an unhappy one. In such case, the owner is always at fault, since he is responsible for teaching the dog what's right, what's tolerable, and what's insufferable. This makes second owners braver than first owners, since they are dealing with a greater, unknown canine-quantity. While it is possible for a first owner to tell the whole story, it is more usual for him to recall only the good things about his pet.

Dogs who do not know and respond to the basic commands are very difficult to train for other deeds, simple or complex. Owners describe them in different ways: stubborn, spoiled, stupid, lazy, troublesome, and plain impossible. Happily, the most impossible dog in town is capable of learning the basic commands. They are fundamental to his learning anything worthwhile and absolutely essential if he's headed for any of the dog sports.

There are five or six basic commands, depending on your personal view of training. Number six is the *stand* command and somewhat irrelevant for the perfect pet. The other five commands are important: *heel, sit, stay, come,* and *down.* That's also the order in which we teach them around here, but it's really a matter of personal preference.

If your dog doesn't know those five, his education has been neglected and there's no time like right now for private tutoring. If he knows two of them, teaching him the other three won't be difficult. The big thing to remember—when teaching more than one of the basics—is to teach the commands one at a time. Forget the *sit* until he has the *heel* down pat, and don't rush him. As the training progresses, most dogs pick up the next command at a faster clip.

In the interests of brevity and avoiding needless repetition, each of the basics is taught via the slip collar-and-leash method, with the dog on the trainer's left, and the leash in the trainer's left hand. With a long leash, hold the excess in the right hand or toss it over shoulder. Each of the verbal commands consists of two words: the dog's name and the command. For the dog's sake, a very slight pause between words is proper. "She must mean me, not some other dog," says Duke when he hears his name. "Oh, yes, now I must lower my bottom," he deduces when he hears the word *sit*.

Here's the easiest way to teach the basics:

"*Duke, heel!*" The object is to keep the dog at your left side, whether you are standing, walking, running, climbing

*"Duke, heel!"*

stairs, or riding a bike. On the command, always start off on your left foot—a motion signal to him. In the beginning, walking ahead at a slow pace is best. Use a loose lead, but tug and tighten to bring the dog back to place when he wanders, lags, or bounds ahead. With each correction and simultaneously, repeat the command words, and praise generously when the dog stays close for twenty feet. The time will come when the dog feels comfortable only when he stays at your side. When he's there, he doesn't feel tugs or tightness around his neck.

For those who like to be different, there's no law pending that would require a pet dog to heel at the master's left side. Thus, if you want your dog to heel at your right side, feel free. Just reverse prior instruction and use your right hand to control the leash.

*"Duke, sit!"* Have the dog stand at your left, turn toward

*"Duke, sit!"*

him, and switch leash to your right hand and hold loose. On the command, press down on his quarters with your open left hand. If successful, repeat, repeat, repeat, and be sure to praise, praise, praise until the student sits without pressure.

Not successful? Don't despair. Start as above, but this time hold leash tight in your right hand. On the command, press down on quarters again, but also tug up on leash to tilt dog's head. If he doesn't sit, he's stronger than you are and you might start thinking about a smaller dog.

*"Duke, stay!"* Dogs seem to resent staying in place just as much as children, so this is sometimes a little difficult to teach and enforce. We prefer teaching this off-leash, and the action begins (preferably indoors) with the dog sitting at heel. That means, of course, that he's sitting at your left side and that both of you are facing front, more or less.

*"Duke, stay!"*

Now things get a little tricky. Do these three things simultaneously: 1) give the command, 2) step ahead, *right* foot first, and 3) swing the palm of your left hand back until it almost touches the dog's nose. If he starts to go with you, just grab his collar, stop him, and put him on a new sit. When he does stay on a sit, be lavish with your praise. When you can walk ten feet from him and he'll sit for ten seconds, it's time to try him outdoors.

*"Duke, come!"* Put the dog on a sit and stay, step off about fifteen feet, turn and face him, and give the command. If he comes, fine. Pet him, tell him what a great guy he is, and then test him at greater distances.

Seven dogs out of ten act as if they have gone deaf at this command. For them, the command words must be accompanied by human histrionics. The trainer claps hands or waves arms or stands on his head or runs off or does anything else that might lure the sitting beast to his side. Eventually, and hopefully before the trainer collapses, the dog will learn to come on command.

However, one dog out of ten will run off in a different direction. A long leash is required for such a beast, but tying

twenty feet of clothesline to an average leash will also serve
the purpose. When the dog doesn't come on command, the
master simply tugs, pulls, or hauls the recalcitrant student to
him, never forgetting to pet and praise him when he arrives.

"*Duke, down!*" Put the dog on a sit, face him, and hold the
leash loosely, so that it loops from his collar to your left
hand. The bottom of the loop should be two or three inches
above the floor. On the command, step on the loop. This

*"Duke, come!"*

won't hurt the dog, but it will bring his head down, and the rest of his body will follow suit. Repeat until the dog gets the general idea without feeling pressure on his neck.

The careful reader will have noted that the open palm of the left hand was used in teaching the stay command. This was a hand signal, of course, and the dog learned it without knowing it. At a distance—as from across the room, yard, or street—the open palm of either hand is the signal for the trained dog to stay wherever he happens to be. Just extend

*Hand signal to drop dog*

either arm waist high, with palm open, and facing the dog. The motion resembles an underhand push that tells him to stay, and words aren't necessary, provided he's looking at you.

Well, there's also an easy hand signal to teach for the down command. As noted, the training calls for the leash to be held in the left hand. On the command, and as you step on the leash, swing the right arm up, palm open. Something like a cop stopping traffic. Eventually, this signal will drop your dog at a distance.

Teaching the basic commands is a lost cause if the owner fails to use them. When a pet dog doesn't hear a particular command for a couple of weeks, there's a good chance that he'll either forget what he's supposed to do and look blank, or dimly remember that something is expected and do the wrong thing.

Keeping the dog *au courant* doesn't mean that he has to run through his basics every day, rain or shine, on a set schedule. But he should be tested on a few every day and at the convenience of the owner. Since the average dog lover walks somewhere every day, if only from one room to another, the dog can be asked to come, heel, and sit, and do all those things without exhausting his loving master.

Not everybody practices what he preaches, but I do, or—to put it another way—my wife does when I don't. She is a firm believer in family traditions, and her favorite one calls for always having five or six Labradors in residence. About ten minutes before she starts mixing the daily ration for them and the kennel dogs, those house dogs sense that the time is close for the mixing ceremony in the kitchen, and that's where they gather. When Evie appears on the scene with the ingredients for their dinners, they rush to greet her and make progress hazardous. "Down!" she'll say, and down they go. "I suggest that you stay right where you are," she'll suggest, and they agree. She doesn't have to sing out their individual names. They have been through this many times, and they know she is talking only to them, even when I'm present. Later, Evie will take all six outdoors, ask all six to sit, and place a bowl of dinner before each sitter. It's chow time and they dive into their dinners. Sometimes I wonder if they could be trained to interrupt their dining on command. I've never tried because I wouldn't want anybody to do that to me.

I wouldn't interrupt any dog that was reading, either, but ours seldom pay me that courtesy. Whenever I sit and read, I can count on the early arrival of at least one house dog. He'll sit in front of me and expect to be petted, and if I don't oblige, he'll use one paw or his head to bat away whatever I'm reading. When that happens, I no longer swear. Instead, I use one index finger to point at the rug, and down goes the dog. I don't say anything, although I did years ago with our first house dogs. Ever since, the new house dogs seemed to have picked up what's expected from observing the veterans. Either that or Labs and I are on the same ESP wave length.

So much for some of the ways we use the basic commands around here on a day-to-day basis. When your dog knows the five simple commands, life becomes simpler for you and safer for him, and he is less troublesome to society. When you walk down a busy street with your dog at heel, he won't be running around in heavy traffic. When he's on a sit and stay, he won't knock down a visiting child. When he stays on a down, you can leave the room and not worry about the roasted turkey on the table. And when he comes to you on command, think how happy your neighbor and her cat will be.

Of course, one must be reasonable and not expect too much from even simple commands. When you want Agnes to sit and stay in a corner of the room while you move the rug and rearrange the furniture, it really isn't fair to say, "Agnes, go to the corner behind the piano and sit there until I'm finished." Far better to lead Agnes to the corner and put her on a *sit and stay*. If she knows her commands, she'll stay out of the way.

THE CRATE

Collar and leash are basic tools and good ones are inexpensive. Basic commands are relatively simple and teachable and their only cost is in time. And then there's a piece of basic equipment that's not so cheap, but worth every dollar.

It's called a dog crate, and I wish I had a piece of the business, because wise dog owners wouldn't be without one and more and more wise people are going in for dogs. There are several styles (solid wood, solid metal, durable wire) and there's a proper size for every dog. I've heard and read a great deal of misinformation about the right size for a particular dog. Well, the right size is also the practical one: big enough for the dog to lie and sit in comfort, but small enough so that he'll be uncomfortable when he tries to stand. If he can't stand, the inclination to relax is greater than the yen to complain.

The style we favor is made of wire and has the look of a small cage. When not in use, the crate can be folded and stored, but most owners keep it set up in a corner of a room. If it's always ready, it will get plenty of usage. I've had one set up in the house for thirty years at an amortized cost of less than a dollar a year. These days, a similar crate for one of my Labs costs about fifty dollars, so it's still a bargain.

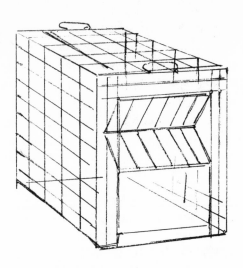

*Most dogs accept a crate.*

Whether a dog is trained, untrained, or still trying, a crate comes in handy just about every day—for the dog, if not for the owner. The average dog doesn't resent it and, if the door is left open, will adopt it as his private cave for occupancy during idle moments, sleeping, and getting away from the vacuum cleaner. And for the dog who travels with his master, the crate can go along as a home away from home. Folded, the crate is easy to stash in or on top of a car. Set up, as in a station wagon, it's a far safer place for a dog than the back seat. If he can't stand, the crated dog won't be tossed around during sudden stops, he won't be able to reach and distract the driver, and he won't be free to stick his head out an open window and get banged in the eye with flying cinders.

If you buy a crate, you'll find it much more convenient for confining your pet than locking him in a room or tying him to a bedpost when you want him out of the way. It's the place to park him when you must be absent for an hour or so and he can't be trusted with furniture, or when he's ill, or when you're painting a wall, or when a friend drops by to show you her new cat.

Acclimating a pup to a crate only becomes a problem when the introduction is hasty and he is forced to stay in it while demonstrating that he'd rather not. After one or two fun visits, any pup takes to a crate the way a duckling takes to water. The owner stays close enough to pet him and play with him for five or ten minutes. Pup or adult, he should not feel that he's being punished or deserted. And in the case of an adult, the introduction should wait until he feels at home and trusts his master.

When the great day comes, the average adult either enters his crate without objection or regards it with hostility. Every effort should be made to con him into the crate without the use of force. Try placing his dinner in the crate (door open, of course), or tossing in his favorite toy, or luring him with a human object, such as a small child. The latter was the only way we were able to get a dog named Boo into her crate many years ago. The big, strong Bouvier rejected all of our tricks and entreaties. Then our youngest daughter arrived on the scene and crawled into the crate. Boo followed, and then she didn't want to leave her favorite child. We never had any more crate trouble with Boo. The command word we use to send a dog into a crate is *kennel*, as noted in Chapter 7.

When it comes to housebreaking a dog completely, a crate is the answer for the beloved pet who never makes a mistake during the day but forgets all his good manners at least once during the night. Call him daybroken, but not nightbroken, and thus incompletely housebroken. The solution is to confine the sinner in a crate at night. He doesn't like to foul his own bed, and will not do so unless he absolutely must. That's one wild instinct that he hasn't lost, and we can be thankful for its preservation. The instinct does not prevent him from messing up a corner of the room if he is free to sleep in another corner.

If the crate method is employed, the most reckless dog can be nightbroken in from one to five nights. Forever after, the now civilized dog will adopt the crate as his personal suite, if its door is tied open. Making the floor more comfortable for sleep and naps entices the rare dog who doesn't grasp the idea. For flooring, I cut a piece of half-inch plywood to size and fit it into the crate. Atop this goes one of Evie's creations: a pillow slip made of tough mattress ticking and stuffed with cedar shavings before the open end is sewn shut. Constant use of this canine bed wears down the shavings and they are replaced about every eight months. The big benefit for the owner is that the cedar scent keeps the dog free of fleas and smelling fresh rather than doggy.

Unfortunately, ticks are not offended by the scent of cedar or anything else. Dogs living in tick country should be examined every day. Remove the little monsters as fast as you discover them. Simply pinch and yank, and be sure to get heads.

If you find a bloated tick, you missed an examination or were a little careless. She (only the female dines on canine blood) will be difficult to remove by pinching, so smother her with a piece of cotton soaked with rubbing alcohol, vinegar, or flea spray. In a couple of minutes, she'll release her grip and can be plucked off. And finally, be sure to destroy ticks that you find and remove. They are too tough to squash between fingers. Bang with a hammer or rock, or burn, or drop into a small quantity of kerosene, or nip in two. Then apply an antiseptic to the spot on the dog's skin where the tick used to be.

*Chapter 4*

# CORRECTING COMMON CANINE SINS

Since he lives under the same roof, it's only natural for a second owner to demand proper conduct from his new dog. The latter, of course, finds the social code confusing. What's fun for him is often outrageous and objectionable to certain people, and antics that his first owner overlooked now irritate you. If dogs were deep thinkers, they would probably reason that people are pretty much the same—generally speaking, that is, but not as individuals.

Your new pet must be educated to your ways and—when he forgets—reeducated. This holds true whether he's a pup or a second or thirdhand dog. And while not on a schedule, the teaching process will be continual—the best-educated and most reeducated dog is going to do something wrong, although not in his own eyes.

When any new or revived canine annoyance surfaces, the owner and not the creator is responsible for correcting it. The sooner the better, of course, and always *at once* when you're the second owner. The dog must be made aware that his new and current boss is for real. Soon does not mean right after taking a bath, washing your hair or finishing an enjoyable phone call. Rather, it means before doing any of those things, and not when you find it convenient.

Here and there on the following pages, this writer recommends such training aides as the cuff, the slap, and the whack, as in the phrase, "Whack his rump." These acts simply reinforce the boss-status of the owner. They are delivered with just enough force to sting and impress, and are not designed to hurt or injure the dog. He really won't mind and will get your point sooner, not later, in certain situations. A whack is not a love tap, of course, nor is a cuff a gentle pat. And an overdone whack drives the dog against the wall, creates fear or hostility, and accomplishes nothing positive. Avoid the overuse of force.

Many trainers insist that the right hand should never punish, since it's the one most owners use to pet and feed their dogs. Consequently, dogs hold right hands in such high respect that their little hearts are broken when said hands are used as corrective agents. The reverse is true for the dogs of left-handed owners, of course.

This is a fine theory, it does no harm, and I'm happy to endorse it. Still, I don't always abide and never will. Such reasoning grants the lovable canine extremely high levels of intelligence, awareness, and feelings, and it calls for continuous consideration on the part of the owner. I feed, pet, slap, whack, hold, groom, and grab with the hand that's handier and none of my dogs seem to care and all of them know who is the boss.

And now, whether you are right handed or left handed or all thumbs, on to some fairly common canine sins and their cures:

THE JUMPER UPPER

Consistency is necessary in both your thinking and training. It is fairly simple to teach Wrecker not to jump

*Cure for leaping*

on people, but weeks of training will be useless if you permit him to jump on those clowns who don't mind, rather enjoy, and might even encourage the greeting. So you don't want Wrecker to jump on anybody? Fine, but be sure to insist that certain people are aware of your desire. You know the ones.

They beat their chests and cry, "How about a kiss, Wrecker? Come on, plant one on my nose." Ask them to kick the habit, then proceed as follows whenever Wrecker jumps:

1. *No!* is the key word. You don't have to use his name, since he'll grasp the idea in a hurry. Accompany the word with action: push him off, bump his chest with one knee, or step on one of his rear feet. Being gentle won't help. He has to remember the contact.

You have to be strong enough, of course, and so do the other family members and friends who agree to help. In the cases of those who lack the will or strength, and those others whom you couldn't possibly ask (complete strangers, unexpected guest, just-out-of-hospital, afraid of dogs, et cetera), consider this:

2. Put Wrecker on leash. When he's about to jump, give him a firm *No* as you snap or tug the leash. If he jumps, repeat the *No* and yank him off target. Follow with a whack on quarters.

It helps enormously if the dog can experience several different knees and a few leash yanks per day, so enlisting cooperative people is a great idea. Three continuous days usually does the trick, but just to be on the safe side with strangers, attach leash and have the dog drag it around as a reminder. Then, should he forget, grab the leash and correct him.

### When A Dog Refuses to Come

The sincerest dog lovers have trouble from time to time with well-trained pets that suddenly act as if they've never heard the *come* command. This happens most frequently with bitches, which are easier to train in the first place. Once trained, males do seem more eager to please and less likely to test tempers. "Sly as a fox" is usually reserved for a bitch and is never a compliment.

The cure for obstinate Suzy might amount to no more than a refresher course on the *come* command, as reported earlier (Chapter 3). Try ten-minute training sessions, twice a day for three days, and don't become desperate if the results aren't satisfactory. It's time to become more particular about your training methods. From now on, it must be one-and-one. Just you and the dog. No audience, and that means not even a silent one.

Start from scratch and indoors. The room can be any size, but all doors should be closed and any other exits blocked. The idea is to have Suzy come immediately on the command word, whether she wants to or not. Show her that you mean business and don't hesitate. If she doesn't move at once, give a strong tug on the leash—and if that's not enough, haul her to you. Whether she arrives voluntarily or with your assistance, be sure to praise her and pet her and offer her a tidbit. Suzy must enjoy obeying you. This indoor training continues until Suzy responds when she's off leash. It seldom takes more than a few days.

Now it's time to go outdoors and work on longer distances. The long lead is required until you think Suzy is trustworthy at over twenty feet. An added advantage of keeping Suzy on lead outdoors is that when she doesn't come when asked, all you have to do is turn and walk away. She'll follow your movement and come to you, so that hauling her to your side won't be necessary. Again, and no matter the means of her arrival, the praise and tidbit remain important. Suzy must be made to realize that you are not going to punish her when she obeys your call, and conning her will help.

For outdoor training, the ideal site would be surrounded by a fence too high for Suzy to jump, but that's not always easy to find. When available, it's a big help when it comes to working the dog off lead. When she disobeys and trots away, she can't go far. Catching her is a must, and so is putting her back on lead. This time, lack of reward will be punishment enough. Then it's back to work.

### The Finicky Eater

The finicky canine, the one who picks at his food and eats very little, is almost always the product of an indulgent owner. Overweight, lack of sufficient exercise, too many table scraps, a constant supply of goodies between meals, and too much attention are among the contributing factors.

*Too many goodies . . .*

A typical case of too much attention is the dog who won't eat unless he is fed by hand.

Granted that he is healthy, gets sufficient exercise, and is fed a wholesome diet on a regular schedule and in proper quantity, a dog just doesn't develop into a finicky eater. Or hardly ever. In times past, we have had a couple of male Labs who just wouldn't eat enough to stay at proper weight. In each case, we conned them into eating more by offering them stale beer (newly opened beer tickles nostrils). Beer contains Vitamin B, an appetite stimulator for man or beast.

For the true, finicky eater, select a wholesome food, determine the proper amount, and offer it on schedule and at room temperature. Remove after fifteen minutes and offer again the next day, adding fresh food if necessary to achieve the proper amount. Do not offer any other food between meals, and make sure nobody else does. Water at room temperature should be available at all times.

This may be strict, but it's also sensible. Within five days, Finicky Fred will no longer be fussy about his food. If I'm wrong, he's not healthy. Check with your vet (see Chapter 7).

Otherwise, don't lose any sleep about when your dog will start finishing off the last crumbs of his carefully prepared and measured ration. So long as he has water to drink, the chances of his deliberately starving himself to death are very, very slim. The canine can go weeks without food.

BEGGING AT THE TABLE

This seems to be an optional sin. Some owners don't mind and I know a few who encourage it. We belong to the opposite school of thought and four-footed members of our family are not allowed around, under, or on the dining table when there's food or drink on top.

The simplest cures are the most obvious ones: just before

you dine, banish the dog from the room or stick him in a crate. The well-trained dog can be put on a down and stay, of course, but he probably won't resist the scents of food for long, and that means several interruptions per meal for you. A firm no and a simultaneous whack on the quarters is the commonest method, but this means *every time* he begs from you or anyone else at the table, and not every guest wants to help you train your dog.

Whatever the treatment, Beggar Bill cannot be cured overnight or in one week. Begging is a strong habit, and your dog must practice total abstinence if he is going to kick that habit. Try not to cheat on Sundays, holidays, and his birthday, and resist his pleading eyes between meals. It will take a long time, perhaps three or four weeks, but you can succeed without resorting to cruelty. Friends of mine who just can't stop smoking have been able to cure their dogs of begging.

"Pay no attention to your dog when he begs" has been popular advice for as long as I can remember. If you follow it, be prepared to make a career of not paying attention. The dog may never stop begging.

## HOUSEHOLD DESTROYERS

The unfortunate thing about canine destroyers of household articles is that guaranteed prevention is never possible. We don't know where they will strike next, if at all, and when. All that we can be sure about is that almost every house dog is going to damage something of value with his or her teeth, and find immense pleasure in the doing. The event happens unexpectedly, and almost always the owner is elsewhere, in another room or another town. "Why did Little Angel do this to me when she's never done anything like this before? And if she had to chew a chair leg, why a Hitchcock? What did I do wrong?"

The above lament and variations are uttered thousands of times every day. The average owner feels a sense of guilt, as if he had forgotten to tell Little Angel that he loved her and please don't eat any chairs. The dog is presumed to have destroyed out of spite or revenge, as if she were a mean, spoiled child. The truth is that boredom and doing nothing do not hold the appeal of chewing, the canine's substitute for solitaire. It's not hunger or vitamin deficiency or anger that causes the chewing. Chairs, rugs, and pillows are just a few of the household articles that any healthy dog views as equipment for a favorite indoor sport.

As canine habits go, this one comes and goes, and dogs frequently go along several years without chewing anything of value other than their daily meals. And then, out of the

blue, they find shoes, coffee tables, plaster walls, and art books too delicious to resist.

The dogs who cause the least destruction are with their owners the most. When left alone, a dog can be trusted not to chew antiques if he has something of his own to chew, such as a meat-scented nylon bone or a rawhide bone. The nylon is more economical for medium-size dogs, since they last for months. A rawhide lasts a few hours or days, depending on the dog. Both are safe, but they should be reserved for those times when the pet is alone. Since the pet dog is bound to chew something, you might as well make the choice for him.

As for the leg on the Hitchcock or anything else that you want to protect from future damage, there are several sprays and powders on the market that are advertised as deterrents, once applied to an article. Their scents linger and are unattractive to a dog. We have never used them, having discovered that a couple of old-fashioned remedies are very effective: bitter apple and Tabasco. Rub a few drops of either on the damaged portion of the leg or whatever, then smear a piece of gauze and place it in the dog's mouth and hold it there for about thirty seconds. Finally, remove the gauze and introduce the dog to the damage. You won't have to repeat.

Should you catch a dog in the act, a strong *no* and a whack on the rump are required. This may not help, but the chances are better than lecturing him ten minutes later.

FURNITURE LOVERS

Small dogs are usually livelier in the house than big dogs, and they are also found more often on sofas, chairs, and beds. As in the begging case, this is perfectly all right in some homes, but not in others, including mine. What follows will interest only those owners who believe that all furniture should be off limits to pets.

The inclination is to rationalize with the dog and say something like "You know better than that, Jimmy" or "How many times do I have to tell you that sofas are for people?" or "Get down immediately or I won't let you lick the dinner dishes." Those and similar entreaties of the moment are ineffective unless the dog is a genius.

When you discover Jimmy lying on the sofa, it's time for him to learn a new command: *"Jimmy, off!"* To teach, grasp his collar and than yank him to the floor on the command. Or, if that seems a little harsh or he's a big dog, substitute the leash for your hand and tug on the command. If he doesn't respond, repeat and pull him off rather than just tug.

It's best to use the word *off*, although the urge to use *down* or *no* is always present. But if Jimmy has had any training, he associates the *down* with lying down, something he's already doing, and he's heard *no* too often in relationship to other things.

With this particular command, there's no need to praise and reward the dog when he hits the floor. He might get the wrong idea and climb right back onto the sofa.

Use the *off* command whenever you find your dog basking above floor level and off limits. I once used it to get a dog down from the mantel, where he had jumped in sheer joy after arriving home from a stay at the vet's.

## WASTEBASKET ROBBERS

These dogs steal discarded items from the basket, rather than the basket itself. The purloined treasures are then chewed or shredded or simply dropped here and there around the home, proving that not all litterbugs look like humans. The simple cure is to catch the thief in the act several times and to discipline him with a firm no and an appropriate whack on the rump. The simple difficulty is that the dog doesn't usually rob and litter when his owner is on hand.

All the retriever breeds are natural carriers of anything that doesn't weigh too much, so we have had our share of Labs who play the game, and most of them have been bitches. The sinner is usually a newcomer in the house, and her peers never join her when she starts robbing baskets. It's as if they know she's sinning and disapprove.

When we discover that there's a new thief in our midst, we temporarily reduce the wastebasket population to a single one and place it where we are not likely to be present during the day. Discarded odds and ends fill the basket, preferably one that the culprit has previously robbed. The suspect is introduced to it and permitted to supervise while we toss two or three selected items into the basket, each a crumbled paper towel that has been treated with either creosote or citronella. An intelligent dog dislikes the scent and taste of either.

Add a couple of treated towels to the basket on each of the next two days. On the fourth day, all the empty wastebaskets are returned to their proper stations, each with a little of the scent of your choice applied to the interior—bottom and sides. Use the baskets at will, but keep using the scent treatment every few days. From start to finish, the method takes about ten days—so long as you don't toss unused portions of steak and lamb into the baskets.

As with all things, the surest way to cure a bad habit is to remove the cause. If you can live without wastebaskets, the problem solves itself, and you can relax until your dog's next bad habit develops.

SPECIAL CITY PROBLEMS

If you live in a big city or visit one with any frequency, you must know that while tens of thousands of pet dogs are paper trained, more are sidewalk trained. City sidewalks are no longer meant for just walking. In the eyes of certain dog owners, that is. Because of them, the ranks of those opposed to the legality of dog ownership in the city keep increasing.

This biggest and seemingly insoluble problem really shouldn't exist at all. The fact that it does reflects on the owners and not their dogs. At any social level, it is never difficult to find people who are irresponsible or helpless when it comes to pets.

Training a dog to use the gutter and not the sidewalk is

not a big deal. Since his body functions are pretty much on schedule, a healthy dog answers nature's call at a certain time or times after each meal. Once a dog's timetable is ascertained, his owner prepares for the coming event by placing paper on the floor or taking him outdoors. In the city, that amounts to putting the dog on leash and taking him for a walk. Many owners are capable of taking their dogs for a walk but they don't know how to guide their pets to the gutter at the moment of truth. The sidewalk is more convenient, but the gutter is more polite and considerate for others—including dog lovers. If you have a friend—are you your own best friend?—who has adopted a sidewalk-trained dog, recommend the following steps:

1. Feed Julia at about the same time every day.

2. Take her outdoors about ten minutes before she's scheduled to answer the call of nature.

3. Walk her on leash and watch for telltale signs: whining, circling, show of anxiety, scenting, positioning. Lead her to the gutter and keep her there until she's finished. And praise her till she gets the idea. Only then are you free to window-shop, talk to friends, or daydream.

The above is sure to satisfy—except in unusual cases, such as the one faced by my friend Maggie. She is an artist who lives alone in Chicago and a couple of years ago she was offered a housebroken Irish Wolfhound by friends who were moving abroad. Big Nick had been raised in the city and was paper trained and Maggie thought that was ridiculous. So she took Big Nick outdoors at the proper times every day, but since he outweighed her and was much stronger, progress was infinitesimal. Over a period of weeks, the giant dog answered nature's calls outdoors a few times, but always in distress and on the sidewalk. The paper-trained canine preferred paper.

Never one to be intimidated by man or beast, Maggie decided to con rather than entreat. Thereafter, she carried an old newspaper along on their walks and placed it on the curb whenever big Nick showed signs of being ready. His excrement, dutifully wrapped in the newspaper, went into the handiest trash can. Dog lovers can be imaginative if they try, and Maggie has found a better way to clean up our cities. Mayors take note.

Big Nick was not afraid to ride in elevators, a fear that is common to many city dogs, small and large. It must be a strange sensation to a dog, with all of his senses telling him that he wasn't whelped for this sort of floating experience. It's very different from natural horizontal movement, so even car-loving canines are often elevator-shy.

Whatever his eventual adult size, a pup introduced to frequent elevator rides will easily adjust to the up-and-down contraption IF he is held in his owner's arms, hears praise and soothing words, and is pleasantly distracted in any other way. He is conned into being confident.

The dog who fears may or may not have had a bad experience in the travel machine. Either way, what he needs is confidence, and it's no trouble with small adults who can be carried in your arms. Treat them like pups. The dog who must stand on his own four feet during the ride needs small talk, constant petting, and play. You must distract both his mind and feet, and try test rides on barely populated cars before exposing him to crowded conditions. Because he's standing, a big dog takes more time. He's experiencing more trauma.

Almost always, fear of elevators is easier to eliminate than love for digging. Since city dogs spend most of their time indoors, their digging opportunities are largely restricted to non-ground surfaces and the results can be irritating and expensive and sometimes irreplaceable. City owners wish their dogs were more understanding. Rugs, upholstery, bedspreads and blankets are the customary targets for indoor diggers, and the damage usually occurs in the owner's absence. It's easy for owners to feel more guilty than angry, as if their pets created the damage out of spite for being left alone. The theory credits the canine with the capability of reasoning at the human level, and it's applesauce.

The indoor dog digs because he's frustrated. The physical act relieves his tensions the way swearing relieves a lost sailor. Since the cause of the digging is frustration, really boredom compounded, the cure amounts to giving the dog something to do besides sleeping when people aren't around, as well as limiting his range so that the oriental rug, best furniture, and silk bedspreads are not available for his pleasure. Thus, a nylon bone for chewing and confinement to the kitchen or a crate are much better ideas than instructive chats and punishments after the fact.

The indoor diggers do not devote their lives to the habit, and can be compared to obese people who stop eating candy. Some will forget all about digging, and some will return to it now and again as the years roll by and they are still left to their own devices for hours at a time.

And then there are the special cases of pregnant bitches. When her gestation reaches the fiftieth day—about two weeks before the whelping—the politest bitch you've ever known could start digging at any hour of the day or night, when alone or in a crowd. This is instinctive. She is preparing a nest for her future pups, and the only way to stop repeat performances is to provide her with a proper whelping box and the right bedding. Outdoors, the same bitch would dig under bushes or sheds or try to find a cave and dig in that.

The city dweller who becomes the second owner of a trained, country-raised dog must be ten times as understanding as the average dog lover. The country pooch has a much harder time adjusting to the city than his opposite number and seldom becomes a satisfactory pet if he has lived in somebody's kennel, a social background that does not prepare any canine for the strange customs, contraptions, and clamors of metropolitan life. Raised in a country home, however, the dog has a very good chance of surviving the drastic switch in environments without becoming a nervous wreck, IF the new city master is endowed with generous amounts of understanding. During the first few months in his new home, Goose Creek Abner needs almost constant human companionship and cannot be trusted when left alone for an unreasonable period (to him), such as an hour. That's when he wants to be somewhere else, as if seeking company, and frustration results. In the animal kingdom, a frustrated dog is one of the very best apartment wreckers. It's not that Abner wants to teach his second owner a lesson. He just doesn't know what he's doing and doesn't care. When it comes to a sense of values, the canine must be in the idiot range.

Since a typical Abner is not paper trained, getting him outdoors at the right time is more convenient than trying to change his relief habits. But if you must paper train the dog, start positioning him on paper at the right times on the very first day. He'll learn, but not soon and not without mishaps.

Easy-does-it when introducing the country dog to the sounds, smells, and traffic that constitute outdoor life in the city. The best times for long walks on lead are when traffic and other action are least. For the dog who finds even minimum confusion too much to take, walking him with somebody else's friendly dog usually does the trick. There's comfort in canine company. It's as if Abner draws confidence from the veteran, city dog and thinks, "This dude isn't upset by all the crazy stuff, so why should I worry?"

The same, canine logic applies to sounds in the night. If Abner is the second owner's only dog, he is almost sure to find some of the new night sounds threatening and voice his opinions. If not reprimanded on the spot, Abner will continue his barking every night for weeks, until he has learned on his own that the noises are harmless. But if a second, city-oriented dog shares Abner's rug, the latter will take his cue from the former and bark infrequently, just often enough to assert his individuality.

Since we can't always hear the noises that disturb our dog, it's easy to decide that a night barker's clamor is unwarranted and that he's "getting even" for a past indignity. If you think that way, you probably don't know that the canine's sense of hearing is acute—at least twice that of man's. Notes of high pitch, ones we cannot and never will hear, are common sounds to him. Other noises that are inaudible to us because of distance are quite distinct to any dog. So when an Abner seems to be barking at nothing, he probably heard something new and strange to him.

# Chapter 5

# CORRECTING STRANGE AND UNPLEASANT HABITS

I've owned a great many dogs in several breeds during my lifetime, and not a single one—past and present—could be rated as perfect. The dog that came closest was a big yellow Lab named Henry. He really aimed to please and was extremely obedient and rarely needed a correction. But he missed pet perfection by a whisker because he did things in his own good time. As a young friend once commented, "Henry should be obedient faster."

Don't get me wrong. I'm not complaining about Henry or any of the others and I've never felt disappointed, not even when I meet somebody who tells me that he owns a perfect dog. The claim never surprises me, nor do I become envious. If I don't run, I will hear more about the perfect dog, always a variation of, "Prettiest bitch you ever did see and from outstanding blood lines. I'm sure you remember her grandsire. Best-of-breed and second in group at Westminster '73. Charlie Westfield handled. Yes, Dolly is a perfect bitch. Everybody says so. However, there is one little thing that she does. Nothing important really, and I thought you might be able to help me. What she does is . . ."

Like every other "perfect" dog on earth, Dolly is perfect to a degree but falls short of being absolutely so. There's no such animal as a perfect dog, and the owner who claims that distinction for his pet is not leveling. Many dogs miss perfection in little ways. Others miss in curious and irritating ways that are more common than dog lovers realize:

### INDISCRIMINATE PIDDLING

Sir Walter Rolly used to be the canine equivalent of a complete gentleman. When your dear friend Susan owned him, he was the very model of good manners and a joy to have in the house. Indeed, Rolly was such a respectable dog and so esteemed by all who knew him that not a member of your family raised even a small objection when you announced that Susan was giving Rolly to you.

By now, Susan has moved to another country and you are wondering if she forgot to tell you something. You have discovered that Rolly has a weakness: he wets the rug at the darndest times! It's all very strange, because sometimes he doesn't even lift a leg, as if he's not aware of his unseemly act. So what's wrong with Rolly? You know he's not shy (Chapter 6) or ill or angry.

Excitement is the major cause. If you'll recall all of the dog's recent mistakes, chances are that they did not occur when the household was reasonably peaceful or normal from his point of view. Does he go wild with joy when you return after an absence of minutes, hours, or days? Does he rush to greet every person who enters your home: friends, guests, the census taker? Is he the life of the party when you entertain? If those are the times he forgets and desecrates the household, the cure depends on calming his joyous responses to you and the others. In your case, don't pay any attention to him for a few minutes. In the case of friends, ask them to follow your example. If that's too much to ask them, stash the dog in a crate for a while or keep him on leash. Those friends, of course, should not bring along their dogs to play with your pride and joy. That amounts to temptation, causes forgetting, and produces another wet spot.

Diet can be the cause of a well-mannered dog's sudden lapses of control. This happens when a dog lover decides that his pet is too special to get along on the foods that are commercially prepared for average canines. Although cute little Lover Boy has been thriving on Hot Doggo and its 22 percent protein, his owner now adds all the boiled eggs, cooked fish, cheese, and other high-protein foods that Lover Boy will devour at one sitting. The owner brags about the dog's remarkable taste buds and can't understand why the pet starts thanking him by leaving unexpected puddles around the house. Well, Lover Boy's bladder capacity is no more remarkable than that of other dogs in his size range, and protein is a great producer of uric acid. The beloved pet must relieve himself more frequently than formerly, and his owner really should leave the back door open.

And then there's the pet who only wets in the house when he's left alone for too long. If he's accustomed to going outdoors at least every four hours during the day, and he's left alone indoors for six or seven hours, who's to blame? The dog's not seeking revenge, he just can't hold the fort all day. Who does?

Finally, there's the dribbler, a variation of the piddler that also commits his deed without intent. Dribbling usually occurs during sleep and naps, and, in polite society, it is regarded as the canine equivalent of bed wetting. If the dribbling occurs every so often and only at night, the cure is to deprive the dog of drinking water around six in the evening and then take him outdoors to relieve himself a couple of times before curfew. This will not work if the nightly trips are too close to a stream, river, or birdbath.

Since it is impossible to train a sleeping dog, the frequent or nightly dribbler becomes a problem. The trained owner takes his dribbler to a vet for examination and solution. The problem may be as simple as a lack of hormones or an incorrect diet. On the other hand, it could be diabetes or a symptom that something is wrong with the kidneys, liver, or bladder. Treated early, there's no cause for alarm. For the unexplainable urinary problem that pops up in a seemingly normal, healthy dog on the sunny side of old age, consulting a vet is a much wiser course than reading a book—including this one.

Those deliberate piddlers known as *markers* are found in the next chapter. Elderly piddlers are discussed in Chapter 8.

## THE OVERSEXED DOG

Breeders sometimes complain with pride about their oversexed canines: the experienced stud dog that can't wait to meet his next mate, or the veteran brood bitch that so loves having puppies she—when not bred—will go through a false pregnancy.

Here we are dealing with the average dog: the only dog in the family. He (she) is called oversexed when his favorite indoor sport amounts to mounting or grasping a human leg or arm and going through shinnying motions. This antic is not approved in proper society and can be extremely embarrassing, as when an honored guest finds himself the object of your dog's attention. The dog does not discriminate as to age, sex, size, friend, or stranger. Any person who will tolerate his nonsense will do.

In the wild, this behavior is used to express dominance. The leader of the pack, for example, hops on another male just to prove he's the boss. That fact of wild life is often used as an excuse by bewildered pet owners, as in "I just can't prevent him from doing that, because the instinct is too strong." Since any pet dog is countless generations removed from his wild forebears, the instinct is too diluted for further discussion.

If a touch of trace remains, we see it in healthy litters of pups and define it as a form of exuberance. At five and six weeks, when pups are able to move about and begin to play with each other, the aggressive ones do climb on (mount) the others. At that stage, it's fun, not a yen for dominance. Once the pup goes to his new home, he continues the fun if permitted to do so. If available, a willing child's leg makes a handy substitute for another pup. Once into puberty, the pet also derives some sensuous satisfaction from the act.

Granted that a given number of pups are permitted to continue the habit—either because the owners don't mind or don't know how to correct it—about half of the pups will cure themselves before the age of seven months. Unless corrected, the others will continue as embarrassments into old age. I never believe the owner who tells me, "I can't understand why this happened. Jazzbo didn't start doing this until he was three years old." Bunk. It always begins in puppyhood and is nourished by permissiveness.

Neutering is often recommended as a cure, but not in this book. Of the many neutered cases I've watched, none of the dogs were cured and only a few seemed to be less oversexed. The owners of even those few didn't trust their dogs around just anyone.

The oversexed dog can be cured, but the training must be consistent rather than random and everybody who comes in

78

contact with the dog must be cooperative. That means keeping him away from people who are unable to help, or putting him on leash when in their company.

Discouragement is the key to success. Let us assume that your dog knows his basic commands. Whenever it appears that he is about to go into his act, put him on a *down and stay* or a *sit and stay*. That goes whether he's giving you the eye or somebody else. Sticking him in a crate when friends arrive won't teach him anything. If he isn't trained, put him on leash and restrain him when he shows a yen. A yank and a firm *no* will suffice.

To paraphrase an oldie, "Dogs should be seen, but not allowed to mount." Constant correction is the only positive cure. Physical restraint, if necessary, doesn't have to be severe. Just enough for prevention. In the long run, the offending pet will get the point and drop the habit. He may or may not resume it on some future date; if he does, reemploy the corrections that worked the first time. The original cure probably took weeks, but the repeat should only take days.

First-time owners of bitches often accuse their pets of being oversexed when they see them playing with and mounting dogs (either sex) from front, rear, or one side. Many adult bitches do this in advance of estrus and some continue right on through the entire heat period, whether or not they've been bred. This is normal procedure, the moon doesn't have to be full, and Cover Girl will again become a model of decorum when her period has run its course.

SNIFFERS AND LICKERS

The sniffers-of-people dog may be just right for hermits, but most owners consider him a social delinquent in the home and at parties or meetings. The dog greets everybody the same way by pressing his nose between their legs as high as possible (if he has the size, against the crotch). I've known a few owners who thought this was funny, but their friends didn't and the ranks of those friends diminished. It's an offensive and almost degrading habit, although the dog means no offense. Why some dogs do it and some don't remains a mystery, although it is not a hangover from puppyhood, and it is true that Bulldogs, Pugs, Boxers, and all other short-muzzled dogs are rarely guilty. Those flat-faced canines do not have the average dog's keen sense of smell and in many cases probably lack normal, bestial curiosity.

Ingenious trainers have developed many new techniques to deal with this problem, but the only one that works all of the time is as old as the *down* and *stay* commands. If he has those two basics down pat, your troubles with Sniffing Joe are over. If he's still uneducated, put him on leash and restrain him from getting close to anyone. You really shouldn't expect other people to cooperate. Prevention over an unspecified period of time is the cure, and punishment (after the act) really doesn't help.

Licking Larry is probably the result of a habit he did pick up in puppyhood and then developed into a fine art under the urgings of misguided people who chanted "Kiss me, kiss me, give me a kissy-kiss, sweet doggie" and then offered praise and reward when he obliged. If certain people are going to be nice to him in return for small dabs of his wet tongue on a nose, chin, or cheek, then Licking Larry is willing to oblige the whole human race.

The first thing a pup feels are his mother's licks: in the very beginning, to get his blood circulating and then to keep him clean. So licking comes naturally to a pup, and even without encouragement he'll lick anything in sight. Sometimes he licks himself, and that's known as self-grooming, and nobody minds. The problem occurs when he develops a liking for licking any exposed part of the human anatomy that is within reach.

Behaviorists will probably argue about why a dog does this until the end of time, but it really doesn't matter if the dog is being aggressive, submissive, friendly, inquisitive, or just satisfying his taste buds. He does it and some people don't like it. If you inherited a Licking Larry, you know why. When he can't find flesh, he's content to lick the clothes you're wearing.

The licking habit never fades away, it just gets worse—unless the owner does something about it. There is no magic cure, and the people the dog sees the most (owner and family or friends) must display cooperation. Most canines won't distinguish between people who like their licks and people who don't. They'll try anybody.

The cure amounts to total discouragement and takes anywhere from a few days to a couple of weeks, so you don't have to devote an entire season to the task. All concerned parties should follow these simple rules:

1. Do not encourage licks. Practice complete abstinence.

2. Anticipate licks and discourage any with a very firm *no*.

3. When dog succeeds, reprimand immediately with a *no* and a slap on his cheek, push him away, and put him on a *down and stay*.

All the above, repeated enough to drive you almost up the wall, will get the point across to Licking Larry that his licks displease you. If he doesn't know his basic commands, stick him in a crate or another room, and see that he learns them as quickly as possible.

And don't relent on Sundays, or the work of many days will go down the drain.

If there's a single pet problem that a dog owner doesn't want to mention to his vet or anyone else outside the family circle, this is it. A canine copographer eats his own feces or those of other dogs, and sometimes those of other animals. The habit is neither instinctive nor generic. It is acquired, and while the most obvious case is environment, nutritional deficiency is sometimes blamed. In any case, there's no cause for worry beyond the stress of personal embarrassment. The dog is not threatened by serious disease.

The dirty habit is often formed during puppyhood and before the members of the litter go to their new homes. If their run or play area is not kept clean between meals, some of the pups will pick up stools as if they were toys and play with them, and that soon leads to eating them. Sporting breeds are instinctive carriers. If a breeder of Cocker Spaniels is irresponsible and keeps the pups in unkempt surroundings, some of the pups are bound to pick up the habit and retain it as adults.

If old stools are in the yard and the owner is absent or looking at birds in a tree, a bored dog might get curious, but not about the birds. This is more likely to happen in winter, when the stools are rigid and easier to hold, but it can happen in any season. It is only possible to prevent copography if a dog is not exposed to temptation. Ideally, the home grounds are kept clean by the owner or his agent. This also makes walking in the yard safer for people.

Once a dog develops the habit, he has a hard time kicking it, and routine training procedures don't help. On the other hand, a slight change in diet has been known to help, and this leads us to the subject of nutrition as a possible cure. If a dog is healthy, happy, gets plenty of exercise and human companionship, dines on good foods, and has no real reason to complain, why does he start eating feces? Is something lacking in his diet? Does he know more about what's good for him than the people who manufacture the food he's fed? How can any brand of dog food be just the right one for all dogs?

Owners who really want to believe that diet deficiency is the answer could be right, but just some of the time. If you suspect that's the cause of your dog's social error, the first thing to check out is the probability that he's carrying worms. Underfed dogs will eat anything in sight, but so will dogs who are at their proper weights and happen to be loaded with hookworms. When worm-free, a dog may forget about his nasty habit.

And he might continue it, leading an expert to conclude that a lack in diet is a strong possibility. The deficiency is usually mineral or vitamin or both. There are several excellent preparations on the market that make up for any such deficiencies, and if nutrition is the only cause, the dog will correct his ways within a month. The various formulas can be mixed into the daily ration, the amount relative to the canine's weight.

Adding small amounts of chlorophyll or butyric acid to a dog's food will change the scent of his own stools and discourage his yen. However, this doesn't help much when other dogs visit the yard and leave their calling cards. I know somebody who solved that problem by sprinkling hot pepper on every stool he found in his yard. This worked in the case of his pet, but it was a little expensive and time consuming, and worrisome when it rained. Eventually and just before moving to another state, he gave the beautiful Irish setter to a cousin. I don't know if the first and second owners are still on speaking terms.

Somewhat related to copography, but not nearly as offensive to humans, is the canine habit of geophagy, which amounts to eating clumps of plain dirt. Again, internal parasites should be suspected. If the habit continues after the dog is known to be free of worms, adding vitamins to the ration almost always solves the problem. The only helpful mineral is iron.

Finding the cause and correcting it is the only way to stop either habit. Training won't help, although simple conning has been known to work in some cases of copography. Dogs who pick up the nasty habit out of sheer boredom were given harmless toys (hard rubber balls, nylon or rawhide bones) to carry around, and they forgot all about the business of collecting and eating feces. That's the way owners of large kennels keep the habit from becoming an epidemic.

### FIGHTERS

The combatants in dog fights are not necessarily vicious, but you can bet that both are aggressive by nature. If one is the submissive type, the fight is over a moment after it begins and no harm is done. That's usually the result of lengthy canine skirmishes, too, unless one dog is really vicious and/or has been trained to fight.

The non-vicious pet dog fights mostly to protect his home territory from a trespassing canine, or to prevent theft of a favorite toy, or for other reasons that are important to him. Most fights are between members of the same sex, and the first impulse of one or both owners is to break up the fight. A foolish owner rushes to the fray shouting such words as "Bad dog" or "No, no" or "Go home" or "Stop, cease, desist" and tries to separate both combatants by grabbing and pulling on the tail or a hind leg of his *own* dog. That advice is found in many books, but I doubt that the authors have broken up any canine battles. Fighting dogs just don't take the time to

identify intruders, and owners have been known to suffer extensive damage.

If your dog gets into a fight that lasts more than a few seconds and you feel the urge to stop it, don't get too close to the snapping dogs. Stay at least five feet away and try to provide a distraction that will catch the interest of the dogs. Pails of water or a steady stream from a hose are excellent choices. Noises won't help, but anything that both dogs feel will, so toss whatever is handy. Indoors, there's usually a chair nearby, or throw a sheet, blanket, coat, or rug over the warriors.

Old-timers in the dog game will tell you that every canine

has to get at least one fight out of his system or he's "not fit to feed." Well, that's hogwash, but there's logic in something else that they say: "Once a fighter, always a fighter." It is valid in the case of a winner. There's something heady about victory.

If your Hercules was a loser or submissive, you can be almost certain that he will not tangle with another dog, not even one half his size. But if he was a winner, then keep an eye on him when he's in the company of other male dogs. Reprimand him when he growls, snarls, or raises his hackles, and be rough about it. He must know that he's not king of the walk and that you're the big boss. This is not the time for sweet talk, petting, and rewards. Should Hercules continue to look for a fight, put him on leash and make him wear a muzzle. Sooner or later, he'll get the idea that you are displeased with his aggressive behavior. He'd rather please you, for you are the dominant member of *his* pack. You are the leader.

The average Hercules will again be a peaceful member of canine society in about two months. Then he can be praised and rewarded when he walks down the street with you and stays at heel and hardly glances at dogs who might want to provoke him.

Will neutering create a submissive attitude and thus act as a preventative? No.

Will mating cure a dog's yen for fighting? No, but it sometimes encourages it.

Does a fighter prefer to brawl with his or her own sex? Usually, unless challenged, and then the size and sex of the opponent won't matter.

# Chapter 6

# MODIFYING PERSONALITY TRAITS

If any fifty canine authorities you care to name agree on one thing, it's that the canine personality is more difficult to change than a human one. You can't really reason with your dog. Oh, you can try, and he might be interested in the sound of your words, but he will never comprehend their logic.

Those fifty authorities would also agree, if pressed, that certain canine personality traits can never be completely changed. Unfortunately, they are the same traits that some owners just can't abide and fail to describe when they find new owners for their dogs. Everything changes for the dog except the personality problem. His second owner is new, the home or apartment is new, and so are the experiences. His offending trait remains.

No matter how much training time is devoted to him, his black trait will not disappear. Still, there's no sensible reason for despair. While the trait cannot be eliminated, it can be modified to the point where it ceases to be a problem. So unless you are an absolute perfectionist—and if you are, it's foolish of you to own a dog—you can reduce the trait to a size that doesn't irritate or offend.

## THE SHY DOG

Shyness has many facets and rates first consideration. The trait is almost always easy to recognize. From puppyhood to old age, the shy ones are never friendly and outgoing. That doesn't mean they are unhappy, but they are still misfits in canine society and ours and find it extremely difficult to adjust to a new environment. Many a second owner has been conned into believing that his shy dog is really suspicious and that love will melt away his misgivings. Beliefs like that are in a class with sweet dreams.

If your dog is shy, he's one of many millions who are making their owners unhappy right now, and chances are that he came into the world with the tendency. Nine times out of ten, shyness is inherited, but that doesn't mean that all the pups in a given litter are shy. Genetic shyness is handed down from the dam or sire or both, and the longer the trait runs unchecked, the greater the severity. Modification is just the reverse. Thus, the younger the shy dog, the greater the chances of reducing his shyness to a mere pittance.

In the world of purebreds, it would be simple to stamp out most inherited shyness if all breeders ceased mating shy animals. The American Kennel Club (the AKC) decreed in the long ago that shy dogs could not be shown. If adherence had been practiced, shy dogs would be far less abundant today. But there are ways to temporarily disguise shyness, and there are show judges who think that dogs are never shy, only embarrassed. So some of the most responsible breeders continue to breed shy dogs who become champions, and the army of unethical breeders remains more concerned with puppy sales than puppy temperaments.

While genetics is usually the cause, a perfectly sound pup can be turned into a nervous wreck if his environment is one of constant stress. The shyness is induced, almost forced on the growing pup, by an owner who has sadly overestimated canine intelligence, capabilities, and potential. The pup's training is hurried, and he's exposed to experiences that would frighten children. He's not mistreated, but he is mishandled and misunderstood. The owner isn't mad. He just seems that way when he's away from the bank, where he's president, and tries to get the most out of his investment in his pup.

And then there is kennel shyness, the result of routine confinement and too little contact with people, and little or no socialization. Understandably, a kennel shy dog doesn't take new people and situations in stride. He doesn't have to live in a kennel, of course. A neglectful owner can create the same conditions by leaving the dog chained and alone most of the time.

A shy dog does curious things, often at inconvenient times, and the degree of his shyness dictates the extent of his repertoire. Several years ago, a young married couple bought a country home near me and looked around for a dog to guard the premises while they were absent. What they wanted was a housebroken dog big enough to discourage any trespassers, and they were delighted to find a purebred Newfoundland pup of seven months, a gift from a friend of a friend who had decided that the big youngster was too much for her small, city apartment. The only drawback was that Butch, while housebroken, had little, mindless accidents on occasion. That was not a cause for alarm, since—according to the donor—the pup's vet had said that the youngster would "outgrow his forgetfulness." A tall tale.

Those little accidents amounted to little puddles that Butch left around the house whenever the phone rang, somebody dropped a pan in the kitchen, a mouse ran across the room, or something else happened that a normal pup would learn to take in stride. When his new owners became irritated and told him that he was a bad dog, Butch cocked his head, wagged his tail, and wet the floor. He wasn't being deliberately bad. He was shy.

The more the owners pleaded with Butch and tried to correct him, the more he seemed to rebel. He would go on hunger strikes and refuse all old favorites and new goodies, but when both owners were away at work, Butch would tear a pillow into little pieces and eat most of them. His shyness was growing, and soon he started nipping hands that reached out to pet him. Now he was a fear biter. Not vicious, though the results were pretty much the same.

By the time this pup was a year old, he had also turned into an incessant barker and the biggest nuisance in my county. When guests arrived, Butch would back off, sit, and bark. If scolded by his owners, he sometimes shut up for five minutes, but not for ten. Let's just say that shy dogs are not always reticent about barking.

Well, shyness cannot be modified in a short period of time, such as a few weeks. And it cannot be modified at all if the dog lacks a great deal of human companionship and constant socialization. Butch lacked both, and the fact that his shyness increased probably surprised his owners. They loved him and cared for him, but they didn't see much of him during the week, they were pressed for time on weekends, and he was rarely exposed to the world beyond their yard.

If your dog is shy, he won't become less so without more of your companionship and gentle corrections, and a better socialization program will help. Constant barkers, of course, are not necessarily shy, and the way to prepare them for a less noisy life is next on the menu.

And if your dog is a purebred and belongs to one of the herding breeds (Collie, Belgian Tervuren, and Shetland

Sheepdog are examples), he may not be as true-blue shy as you think. In the long ago, those breeds were developed to be suspicious and sometimes that built-in trait remains and can't be erased. So if you own a herding dog and he's aloof with strangers and sometimes barks at your new friends, he's only doing what comes naturally. But if he trembles or wets the floor when they approach, or if he nips the hand that is extended to pet him, he really is shy and you've got a problem.

## The Noisemakers

Does Silly Millie bark every time you wear a certain hat and does she absolutely refuse to shut up until you have removed the indignity to her good taste? If that's the problem, burn the hat, give it away, or don't wear it in her presence. That's called removing the cause, and it's the simplest way to stop a dog from barking.

Unfortunately, habitual noisemakers bark at almost anything, and it's impossible to remove all the known causes. From a dog's point of view, the vocal exercise usually has meaning as an expression of joy, excitement, or alarm. And at other times he sounds off for reasons—so far as we can discern—that are completely irrational, unless we grant the canine enough intelligence to know the best way to irritate people.

In my long and unfinished career with habitual barkers, the best correction has been a combination of the verbal and the liquid: "Jumbo, no, no, no, no!" and a simultaneous, goodly amount of water in the face. Outdoors, the goodly amount is a pail of water, or five or six quarts. Indoors, and out of respect for furnishings, a glass or cup of water is employed. The water method does not harm the dog, but it does surprise and offend him, and he is more apt to remember than forget. As time goes on, an empty pail or cup will bluff him into silence.

Two words for those who have just decided to refine the system by using a water pistol: Forget it. The amount of water isn't sufficient, and aiming isn't easy. The water must splash into the dog's face. To be sure of that the pistol must be held close, and then it becomes an ineffective toy that the victim might grab and discard between barks.

If you are reasonably consistent, and that means at both convenient and inconvenient times for you, your noisemaker will be a quiet joy around the house within a week. Up in the future, he's almost sure to forget his silent manners and resume barking with the old abandon. Whenever that happens, depend on a few splashes of water in the face to remind him that the virtue of silence is dryness. The water cure, then, is not guaranteed to last forever.

The only permanent one that does last forever requires the services of a vet. Surgery can remove the capability to bark, but this is a cure for desperate situations and dog lovers who approve are rather rare.

Among the world's many pure breeds, only the Basenji is naturally barkless, although he's not mute. He talks in a singsong manner, a yodel sort of chortle. The perfect choice for the dog owner who lives in a thin-walled apartment with complaining neighbors on each side.

### The Operatic Canines

If there's any dog more irritating than the habitual noisemaker, he has to be the howler, the beast with operatic tendencies. He usually reserves his best efforts for late at night when he's reasonably sure his owner is asleep. Again, a splash of water in the face is the best antidote for the adult howler—short of moving the dog and his bed into your bedroom.

*A little night music*

While effective, the water method is inconvenient for owners, since it means crawling out of bed two or three times per night. It is very inconvenient in the case of the outdoor dog singing in his kennel run. Acquiring another dog so that he can have a playmate usually works, but not for long. After a few nights there are two howlers. Canine opera is contagious.

Our indoor dogs are not a problem in this respect. All those in residence have their appointed places in the master bedroom. They do not howl when conditions are normal, but conditions are abnormal when a bitch is in heat elsewhere on the place. At such times, males are almost sure to howl wherever they are, and those present indoors move outdoors. A lovelorn male knows a great number of ballads, water in the face only serves to refresh him, and nothing else seems to hush him. We suffer less in winter, when only one window is open.

If he's left alone at night in a brand new environment, a new dog is almost sure to howl. His musical lament relieves his confusion and is understandable, but it becomes a nightly habit if not checked. In the same situation, a pup whines and barks and finally howls. He's a baby and afraid, but easy to distract, and steady sounds comfort and quiet him and lull him into sleep. Try the radio, a loud ticking clock, hamsters on a wheel, another pup, water dripping into a pan, or stick him in a crate and bring him into your bedroom and talk to him as you would to a baby—without threat.

### CAR CHASERS

Chasing cars is the canine substitute for Russian Roulette, but the dogs are not concerned. There's joy in the

chase—and it's so much fun scaring the daylights out of drivers and observers.

Again, the water correction is the simplest and most effective to apply. Keep in mind that the water must hit the dog full in the face, and that there must be enough of it to make an impression. Several quarts in a pail are recommended, and since the water will be tossed from a moving car, carrying an additional supply will prove a convenience—in case of misses.

A car and driver are required, as well as a passenger who serves as the tosser. The latter could be you, or a friend. And just to be on the safe side, find a site that's devoid of other moving vehicles. Don't call to him, but permit the dog to chase the slow-moving car and then receive a mighty splash of fresh water in his face. After a few such experiences, even avid car chasers usually get discouraged and retire from the sport. Command words aren't necessary. While water and blank pistols are highly recommended (by others), they are also highly ineffective.

If a dog knows his basic commands, of course, he can be restrained from chasing cars. If he's still untrained, he can be kept on leash or in a confined area when outdoors.

Close to four million dogs are killed every year on this nation's streets and highways. This sad fact is often regarded as proof of a canine surplus, but doesn't it really reflect a surplus of irresponsible owners?

THE ROAMERS

Not all of the dogs killed on the roads are car chasers. Some are reckless roamers who try to cross roads in heavy traffic. If successful, they continue to run such risks as being shot, poisoned, or stolen.

Lectures, advanced training, and a change of diet will not

deter a dog from roaming. Dogs roam because they are looking for fun, curious about scents carried by the winds, or just for the heck of it. And then there are special causes for roaming: the male who has received the airborne message that a bitch is in heat on the other side of the hill, and the bitch in heat who runs off with her new admirers, all males. But whatever the causes, one condition remains constant: the roaming dog—accidentally, temporarily, or customarily—is permitted to run free.

The only sure correction is confinement. When he's alone outdoors, that means a fenced yard or a kennel run, not tying him to a tree or post. Any dog needs and deserves at least a little running room.

This brings us to neutering as a cure, but only because somebody out there is wondering about the advisability at this moment. In theory, both castrated males and spayed bitches prefer the comforts of home to roaming. In practice, the surgery works with many dogs who weren't roamers in the first place, so neutering amounts to preventive or precautionary action. On the other hand, spaying does not deter the veteran roamer, and castration does not always cause a male to lose interest in the opposite sex. Let it be said the surgery can remove the power to reproduce, but it can't take away the joys of roaming and dreaming.

Punishment does not cure the roaming dog, since it must be applied after the deed, when he's found or returns of his own will. He has to figure that if he's being punished for anything, it's for coming home. It just isn't the same as spanking a child for coming home late.

All of this advice about roamers did not convince a certain Princeton professor whom I count among my dog-loving friends. In an effort to discourage his dog Sugar from roaming, the instructor of tomorrow's leaders devised a unique form of non-physical punishment: upon returning home, Sugar was told she was a very bad dog and was not fed for twenty-four hours. This happened many times. While the punishment did not stop Sugar from roaming, she became an expert at overturning the garbage cans of neighbors. The professor solved both problems—the new and the old—by giving Sugar to a friend in Arizona. "I just couldn't confine her," he confessed. "Dogs should be free." A popular and foolish thought.

TERRITORIAL MARKERS

The marking habit is something that the domestic dog still has in common with his very ancient ancestor the wolf. The sexually mature dog marks his territory (home grounds) by dousing certain objects with his urine, and all other dogs who happen to pick up the scent are supposed to know that they are off limits. Uric acid has remarkable staying power in any weather, and the scent of one dog's urine is different from any other dog's. If that seems unlikely, consider what we know about human fingerprints, and humans greatly outnumber dogs.

While all dogs mark, males are usually much more active than bitches and a bred male (stud dog) marks as if it were his duty. Fortunately, most marking occurs outdoors and average trees, bushes, poles, and fence posts withstand the baptizing in good shape. Corrections are in order when and if the dog extends his marking activity to lawn furniture, bird baths, garden tools, and the front door. Most housebroken dogs do not mark indoors. Still, it does happen when the situation calls for it, as when your friend visits and brings along his new dog to meet your Atlas, and the latter wants the strange canine to know who owns the piano. And a stud dog at home can be almost counted upon to mark

97

when the visiting canine is an adult bitch.

The marking problem cannot be entirely abolished, but you can stop a dog from marking particular objects by staying close and on the alert as he nears whatever you have deemed immune. He will show his intention by preliminary sniffing or working his hind legs into appropriate positions. At that moment, grab him, cuff him (under the jaw), and shake him (if he's not too big), all to the thunder of your own voice shouting "No, no, no!" If you are a little late, grab him during the marking or at its conclusion. The unaccustomed rough handling and vocal volume will impress him, and repeating the correction is seldom necessary. So once is usually enough, but that translates into once per sacred object.

There are several sprays on the market that some owners use on specimen shrubs and patio tubs in need of protection from uric acid. While the best of the sprays are effective, the spraying itself must be repeated at intervals, the method is costly, and I've seen clever dogs turn their heads away from a sprayed juniper and mark contemptuously.

And then there are the chemical wicks that are placed near whatever is off limits. These do discourage some small dogs and most cats and are certainly less obvious than fencing, the next best thing to training. If you haven't checked on the cost of fencing lately, do so. It will give you one more reason for training.

## MOUTHERS AND NIBBLERS

A mouther holds your wrist or hand between his or her jaws. The dog does not apply pressure unless you try to detach yourself, and sometimes he'll try to lead you away from where you are, but not to any place in particular. Animal psychologists have not decided on the cause for this behavior, although the field has been pretty well narrowed to affection, possessiveness, or leadership (of the person). Perhaps all three causes are involved, although many breeders (including this writer) prefer to simplify the mouthing habit and label it as a hangover from puppyhood.

The brood bitch, if she has the true maternal instinct, constantly washes her pups. In this process, she licks and mouths them, and by their fourth or fifth weeks, the pups mouth each other as a form of play. Many adult dogs continue to play with each other in this way, although more bitches seem to cling to the habit. The dogs are always friendly with each other and people.

Some owners don't mind the mouthing trick and others dislike it very much. If your dog is a mouther and you really don't mind, so be it, but consider this: in the long run, your dog is almost certain to extend his favor to your friends and other people he meets, and not all of them will think your pet is cute. Indeed, those who are afraid of dogs might faint.

If you want to discourage Tallulah's mouthing habit, a little practicing will come in handy. Find the best way to open her closed jaws a little with one hand. You will probably find that she will open her jaws when you apply pressure where they are hinged (thumb and index finger, one per side). Since you won't be able to do this with the hand (wrist) being mouthed by Tallulah, practice with each hand.

The next time she begins to mouth your wrist or hand, scold her. If she doesn't withdraw her jaws, continue scolding as you use your free hand to open her jaws enough to remove your captive hand. Follow through immediately with several slaps on her cheeks and refrain from paying attention to her for at least an hour. If Tallulah doesn't mouth again, she's a very bright dog and belongs in the movies.

*"Tallulah, no!"*

Mouthers seldom ask for more of this treatment on the same day, but they will keep trying for about a week and must be corrected each time. A few dogs swear off mouthing forever, but the average dog has to go through a refresher course once or twice a year.

The correction and the time limits are the same for nibbling, an advanced form of mouthing displayed by friendly dogs who don't know their own strength. When a nibbler holds your hand, you feel the pressure of her teeth in brief, irregular tempo. The nibbles aren't enough to pierce the skin, but they have been known to frighten the daylights out of a stranger.

Lessons for either a mouther or a nibbler are not effective unless all the important people in the dog's life cooperate. If your dog qualifies, those people he might approach to play the game should do as you do, or at least scold and refrain from petting.

The nip and the bite are different degrees of the same damage, with the nip being the lesser and not likely to leave a permanent scar. In the dog game, we don't differentiate between nippers and biters and rate them delinquent in temperament and unsuitable as pets. They are what they are because of inheritance, environment, or training, or any combination. In a word, nippers and biters are *mean*, and they can't be counted upon to bark before swinging into action. Nippers can turn into biters, but the reverse is not true, and that may be because the taste of blood is exhilarating. As considered here, neither type should be confused with fear biters (shy dogs) or mad biters (rabid). There is still no known cure for the latter and they are always destroyed.

Biters are completely unpredictable, in the sense that they don't always discriminate as to whom or what they damage. Some bite their owners, and some bite everybody in the family except the owner, and others prefer the owner's friends, relatives, and acquaintances. Why dog lovers continue to feed and pamper the canine misfits known as biters is a mystery that can become very expensive. The owner is always responsible for medical and hospital costs, as well as possible damage suits. It does not matter if the canine biter inflicted his damage at home or at large, and trespassers and thieves have as much right to sue as postmen, paperboys, and plumbers.

It is not possible to reform a biter completely, and training to reduce the frequency and fervor of his mischief is best left to a professional trainer—if one can be found. The treatment is long, abusive, and very expensive, and I don't know of a pro who guarantees a cure. If you insist on keeping a biter and can't find or afford a willing professional trainer, by all

*101*

means limit his opportunities to bite, take advantage of every opportunity to pray, and don't invite me to your next party.

Nippers are a different story, for they can be taught to forego their favorite hobby most of the time. During moments of stress, as when somebody excites, surprises, or threatens him, the reformed nipper tends to forget the rules. He also reacts when old temptations reappear: he sees somebody running down the street, or he is teased by a child he never did like. Insomuch as possible, those stresses and known temptations should be avoided.

To reform a nipper, he must be forced to associate unpleasantness with his own unpleasant action. This calls for instant, harsh action. Very firm vocal reprimands (any words will do) accompanied by cuffs and slaps. Whacks on the rump won't help. Only the jaws are important.

Next, the dog is restricted to his crate (or tied), and completely forgotten (he thinks) for a couple of hours. He should not be isolated. The crate (or where he's secured) should be in view of normal household activities.

The rough treatment won't mean a thing unless it is dished out by the owner. Simple enough when your dog nips you, but how about when he nips somebody else and you see it happen? Rush to the scene and act as if he had nipped you, then place him in custody. If somebody else starts pushing him around, he might nip again!

Forgiveness, changes of diet, and neutering do not restrain the nipper, but one trick has been known to work with pups. After each nip, this calls for vocal reprimands and placing the pup's front paw (right or left) between his jaws, then holding the jaws shut. Does the pup realize he's hurting himself? Who knows? It doesn't really matter if it works, and the pup isn't injured.

*Restricted but not isolated*

So it's possible to cure the very young. As for adults, Fu Manchu put it best: "The wise never put their complete trust in nippers, and only fools tolerate biters."

*Chapter 7*

# OBEDIENCE FOR SECOND OWNERS

There are more varieties of dog lovers than dogs, and one of the commonest is the EM, short for Excuse Maker. Members of the club are not up to training their dogs to do anything much. While they may know the rudiments of training, they are simply incapable of applying the knowledge. A typical EM does not admit his lack of talent and tries to hide it with an assortment of excuses, including lack of time and a personal admiration for his dog's free spirit. Otherwise, an EM is just like any other dog lover, and—if his dog is not present—it's impossible to pick an EM out of a crowd.

Members of the variety with money to spare have always been able to find relief by engaging the services of a professional dog trainer who knows how to get results and considers his modus operandi a trade secret. Years ago, the professionals were only found in the big cities and wealthier suburbs, locations where EM's were found in abundance. These days, wherever you are, there are pros in both the hills and valleys, and some will even make house calls.

If you are an EM, that's the easy (and costly) way to train

*104*

or retrain your dog, granted that the pro you select has substance to match his advertised promise. The trouble comes in the long run, a matter of weeks or months. The dog has been reformed, but not you, and his good manners dissipate as he senses that you and your modest talent haven't changed. When it dawns on the dog that the pro is not hiding behind every door, his good old days will return, and you are back on square one.

For EM's and all other owners who can't seem to get the desired results teaching solo, obedience training schools are almost always the ideal solution. While they have been in existence for almost fifty years, the number of schools has increased dramatically in the past fifteen years and it is no longer difficult to find a good one wherever you live in the United States. Some of the schools are privately owned, others are sponsored by social, civic, kennel, and Obedience clubs, and still others are a part of adult education programs.

The success of the schools is based on the theory that some owners need as much training as their dogs. Or to put that another way, the owner needs to be trained to train his dog. All this instruction is conducted by the group method: owners and their dogs attend class together and learn together. At a typical school, a course lasts eight to ten weeks and costs twenty to thirty dollars. One session per week (usually in the evening) with daily practice at home advised for best results.

Most schools welcome all dogs (purebred and otherwise), as long as they are not vicious and are at least six months old, an age qualification that has certain drawbacks. The most impressionable period for any canine is his first few months, particularly from two to six. He is not set in his ways, his curiosity overfloweth, and he's very open to suggestion. It's a fine time to teach him what's right before he has the chance to develop wrong habits on his own. So now a growing number of schools are offering KPT (kindergarten puppy training) for young pups. The canine students are cajoled into responding to simple commands, perfection is not expected, and owners seem to have as much fun as the tail waggers. A side benefit for the pup is early socialization (new sights, sounds, scents, people), and a great benefit for the owner is the assurance that the pup will be pleasanter to live with up ahead.

Almost all of the established schools offer these classes:

BEGINNERS

The dog is taught his basic commands and anything else the instructor feels the owner can handle. The older the untrained or mistrained dog, the more set in his ways and the more difficult it is to bring him in line. Still, it is always less difficult with the group method. The alert owner is doing the right things and the stubborn dog always seems more cooperative in the company of his peers. It could be group magic, but it's probably ego.

By the time a dog completes either KPT or Beginners, the instructor and other experienced handlers (on hand to train their dogs via the group method) have a very good idea about the chances of the new graduate and his owner in the sport of Obedience. This is the next best thing to a canine Olympics, and some people think it's superior, since the dogs win degrees in higher education rather than medals. Granted that a dog has above average IQ and can be conned into applying it, he can win as many as four degrees and the title of Obedience Champion—provided his handler has mastered the art of training. To succeed, the dog and his owner must work as a team.

Since the sport is approved, recommended, and regulated by the AKC, only purebreds are eligible in Obedience, and they must belong to one of the 131 recognized and listed pure breeds. Further, a given purebred must be registered by the AKC, at least six months old, neither vicious nor lame, and neither completely deaf nor blind. Those are also requirements for showing (breed ring), but there all similarity ends. It's perfectly okay for an Obedience dog to be neutered and he doesn't have to meet any of the specifications dictated by his breed standard. Thus at any Obedience trial it is not unusual to see a white German Shepherd dog, a spotless Dalmatian, a spayed Collie bitch, a Boxer wearing uncropped ears, a Vizsla with a long tail, and a happy-looking Basset Hound. Yes, beauty is appreciated, but only brains count.

Obedience trials are held all over the country and in every season. The ones leading to the degrees are licensed by the AKC and held in conjunction with dog shows or separately. Indoors and outdoors, the annual grand total in the United States now is about fourteen hundred.

One would think that an experienced owner-handler would be able to train his new Obedience dog at home and not go through the school routine again. Most veterans would agree, but many of them continue training at the schools along with the newcomers. Obviously, the group method is great for both actors and dogs. These are the advanced classes offered at most training schools:

NOVICE

Tutoring for the six exercises a dog must perform to earn the degree of Companion Dog (CD). Each exercise calls for instant obedience to one or more basic commands, each is worth 30 or 40 points, and a dog that performs per-

*Novice. Heel free.*

fectly (in the eyes of a judge) scores 200. A "proper" score of 170 or better qualifies for a leg, and three legs at three different shows amount to the CD degree. An "improper" score of 170 or better qualifies only for another try on another day. Impropriety occurs when a dog picks up fewer than half the points up for grabs in a given exercise. For example, heel free (heeling off leash in a certain pattern) is worth 40 points, but a sloppy performance could earn only 19, or less than half. If perfect in all other exercises, the dog will score 179 on the day, but it won't get him any closer to the degree.

OPEN

Practice for the degree of Companion Dog Excellent (CDX). This trial consists of seven exercises, each worth 20, 30, or 40 points and more complicated than those found in Novice. On command, the dog does a few new things: retrieving, jumping (high and broad), and dropping to ground on signal as he responds to the *come* command. Again, 200 is the perfect score, a proper 170 or better is worth a leg, and three legs earn the CDX degree.

*Open. Jumping.*

## UTILITY

Rehearsals for the six exercises the dog must perform properly to earn what amounts to a graduate degree: Utility Dog (UD). Each exercise is worth 30 or 40 points, 200 is the perfect score again, a proper 170 wins a leg, and the usual three legs for the degree still stands. This is the only degree calling for both the use of hand signals and the dog's scenting powers. When your dog becomes a UD, it's okay to consider yourself a great trainer. It will not be necessary for you to listen to others or read books.

These three degrees must be earned in the order named. Thus, Dapper Dan CD is eligible for a try at his CDX, and Dubious Dora UD has already earned her CD and CDX degrees. But both dogs, as well as Wild Willie CDX and Cute Clara (who has no degree) can have a go at this degree:

## TRACKING DOG

In Obedience circles, this is known as the TD and, unlike the others, it is a one-shot affair. In the opinions of two judges, the candidate passes or fails the test. To pass, the dog must follow the fairly fresh trail of a stranger for at least 440 yards and then find an article (wallet, glove, et cetera) hidden by that person. The mission must be accomplished without guidance and with reasonable attention to the business at hand. A failing dog loses the trail or chases a rabbit or loafs along the way.

Since virgin unused territory is a must, tracking tests are held apart from dog shows and Obedience trials. Dogs of most breeds can cop the TD, with the exception of those with subpar scenting powers, such as the flat-faced Pug, English Bulldog, Boxer, and English Toy Spaniel. Only a few training schools offer help, but local tracking experts

aren't hard to find through kennel and Obedience clubs, and most libraries carry literature on the subject. A TD dog isn't much help around the house, unless you're in the habit of misplacing things, and tracking has been mentioned here to complete the story of Obedience degrees. Almost.

Prior to 1977, a UDT (Utility Dog Tracker) had all four degrees and no other Obedience mountains to climb. Since 1977, there's been a title: Obedience Trial Champion. Only UD and UDT dogs can wear the title, but first they must win it, and that means competing again in Open and Utility trials. A dog wins championship points by achieving high scores (first and second place) and 100 such points, under certain criteria, make a new champion. The first two titles went to Golden Retrievers.

Overall, the best-trained dogs in America own one or more Obedience degrees. In many cases, their owners were helpless when it came to training—before they attended an obedience school. I've seen it happen time and time again. The group method really does help and never seems to hurt. Perhaps it's just a matter of climbing into a boat with other dog lovers, sharing miseries, and solving training problems together.

No matter where you live in this country—with the exceptions of Hawaii and Alaska—Obedience trials are held within driving distance of your home on most Saturdays and Sundays. When the nearest trials are a bit too distant, there are usually match trials—really practice runs for the real thing that are held by various dog clubs for the benefit of newcomers—closer to home. However, this general schedule does not hold true during the three-week period that begins on the weekend before Christmas. This holiday from canine activities is not appreciated by all dog fanciers and it may disappear any year now.

The growing enthusiasm for the sport of Obedience is sure to intensify when more young dog lovers get into the act, and that's bound to happen. The trials are fun, they are great places to meet and make new friends, and the awards for the highest-scoring dogs in each class include ribbons and trophies and often cash. In addition, there are usually special awards for the highest-scoring dogs in specific breeds.

Although the sport's rules and regulations call for dogs to be at least six months old, the age range for handlers is wide open. So a handler is never too old or too young—so long as he's strong enough to control the dog. I've seen very few handlers under the age of seven, and in the seven to sixteen set, girls outnumber boys. It's not that the boys can't train their dogs, they just hate to look silly in public when their dogs goof.

How important is Obedience for second owners? Quite possibly, it's more important for them than first owners. The more *time* spent together, the more the harmony between second owner and dog, and the better the chance of solving any pet problem. That's active time, as in training, or going places and doing other things as a team. Passive time, as when owner watches TV. and the dog sleeps at his feet, is pleasant and relaxing, but not productive. When success at the trials is the goal, owner and dog must really get to know one another.

## MORE COMMANDS

When a dog has mastered the basic commands to a respectable degree, he is ready to learn a few worthwhile commands that are not taught in training schools and are seldom mentioned in dog books. The worthwhiles vary from home to home, in that one person's idea of a complete pet dog differs a little from the concept of another owner.

A worthwhile command suits the convenience of the owner and satisfies a purpose or a whim. Once learned, the dog fits into the owner's lifestyle a little more and proves once again that he's willing to please. These are some of the commands that have made living with dogs underfoot a happier experience for us:

*Kennel:* The single word *kennel* is used to send a dog ahead of me, whether I intend to follow or not. The dog goes into a kennel run, a crate, a car, the next room, or the vet's office. The appropriate gate or door is always open, of course. My kind of guy doesn't expect the impossible from dogs. Just from dog lovers.

Approach the opening with Jezebel at heel. Stop at the threshold, but send her through it with the command *"Kennel!"* and a sweep of the arm in the right direction. If my command word seems inappropriate, substitute a word of your own—perhaps *go, proceed, enter,* or *charge*—but be consistent. Using the dog's name first is optional. Either way, most dogs continue through the opening and should be praised. Put a difficult dog on lead and pull her through the doorway on the command. Or, if you are sufficiently athletic, pull her through without going through yourself. Small dogs can be lifted.

In due time, the verbal command can be dropped, but not the arm sweep. The latter can be changed to a wave of the hand, and later to a pointing finger. All this does take practice, but it should not be routine practice. Just keep using the command when it suits your convenience, rather than ten times in three minutes. The command is not designed to work at a distance, such as across the room, the yard, or a street.

*Hold:* This command serves two noble purposes: it gives the dog something to do, and it gives the owner a third hand. I use the *hold* for assistance in carrying in the mail or packages from the car, for keeping a tool handy when I'm building or fixing, and for holding a basket so that I can use both hands for berry picking.

Many dogs will hold anything that's presented to them. The trick is to convince the dog to keep his grip for a desired length of time, and this is accomplished by practice and with praise. Make him hold the object by using your hand(s) to keep his jaws clamped sufficiently tight. No other discipline will work as well. The accompanying petting and praise will eventually convince him that holding is fun, not work. On that day, you might find that you can get along without the command word. Simply offer the object to be held to Handyman Harry and he'll wrap his jaws around it.

To avoid unnecessary remorse, it's always wise to pre-determine whether your dog has a soft or hard mouth. All sporting breeds are supposed to be softies, in the sense that they can retrieve shot game without damaging or breaking the skin of the victims. Thus, any spaniel should be able to carry a fresh egg without cracking the shell. *Ho-ho-ho.* Soft and delicate articles should not be entrusted to hard-mouthed dogs, including many dogs in the sporting breeds that belie their reputation. Ah, those dingbat breeders again.

Any dog that becomes expert at holding and carrying objects of your choice can develop a go-fry-ice attitude. Handyman Harry becomes so proud of his accomplishment and is having so much fun that he refuses to surrender the object he's carrying. The best remedy follows.

*Drop it:* On the command *drop it*, use thumb and fore-finger of one hand to apply pressure on jaws. Naturally, the free hand removes the object from the opening jaws and—always—petting and praise follow. Scolding will make Harry think that he was wrong in not holding on for dear life.

A local variation and perhaps an improvement of this command is *drop it, please.* This is Evie's invention and she claims it gets quicker results, but we have never kept records. It could make the difference with a polite dog. She says.

Please note that the dog's name is not used first when giv-ing these commands, which is just the opposite of Chapter 3. When you are working one-on-one with a single dog, and he already knows who's boss, he must realize that you're talking to him. Up close, and unless other dogs are present, his name is superfluous.

*Fetch:* When your dog picks up something and carries it to you, he is fetching—more or less. A proper fetch is performed on command and amounts to a total act. On the command *fetch*, Harry picks up an object, holds and carries it directly to you, and drops it into your extended, open hand.

In the beginning, fetching is really the game of retrieving. For a pup, use something soft, such as an old sock stuffed with rags. A small boat fender is fine for an older dog, and can be used on land or water. Whatever the object, make sure its size and weight are handy for the dog. Handy? Is jawy a legitimate word?

The lesson starts with a little teasing. Wave the object before Harry and permit him to smell it, but not grab it. Then, when he has his eyes on the object, toss it about ten feet and use the command *fetch*. Harry should run to it, pick it up, carry it to you, and drop it in your hand—all without another word from you. If he doesn't, he will, but he'll also need help along the way with such other commands as *come, hold,* and *drop it.*

Dogs often become quite fond of the fetching game, and some want to play at it far into the night. Avid players keep bringing things to their masters in the hope that the things will be thrown. Obviously, the game is more beneficial for city dogs. Good exercise in a small room.

An experienced fetcher will pick up any properly identified object, tossed or untossed. Just point to it, say "*Fetch*," and he'll deliver it to hand. On her daily rounds of the house to put things in their place, Evie's unsalaried help is always a fetcher. Over the years, the dogs have saved her millions of steps, bends, and reaches. They have saved me· countless steps, too. When my wife asks me to bring her something, I give it to a dog, she calls out the command, and he delivers

*"Fetch!"*

the something to her. That's why I call this a very worthwhile command.

### General Health

You can train until you're blue in the face, but if there is something physically wrong with the canine student, he won't feel much like learning much of anything.

As second (or third or fourth) owner, you are automatically responsible for your dog's health and you can't always tell about that from just looking at him. Hopefully, he was in the pink of condition upon arrival, but the real proof of the pudding would be a veterinarian's certificate attesting to preventative innoculations (shots) and other matters. It's more trustworthy than the assurances of the first owner, who is seldom certain about dates.

Too many second owners don't understand that the "permanent" shots to prevent the occurrence of the deadly canine diseases of distemper, hepatitis, and leptospirosis are effective for only a year and that an annual booster shot is needed to continue the protection. And thus far, only a small minority of dog lovers are doing anything about heartworm, another canine killer that has escaped confinement in the southern states and gone national. A simple blood test tells the story: if the dog is free, there's medication to keep him that way, and if he has heartworms, the chances of saving him are good—if his case is not severe.

To be on the safe side, a dog should also be tested for the commoner worms (round, hook, whip, tape) every six months and treated at home (a simple matter these days) if necessary. Heartworm is handled differently from all the other internal parasites and the preventative medication (tablet or liquid) is given daily year round, or—at the very least—for the duration of the local mosquito season, plus six weeks. We prefer the liquid form, since it's so easy to give. Just mix it into the dog's dinner.

And then there's the matter of rabies. The innoculation is good for two or three years, depending on type. It is a must in some places and a good idea everywhere, including cities. There's no cure for a rabid dog. He must be destroyed.

When you keep your dog up-to-date on his shots, tests, and medications, he'll stay in shape and remain immune to a long list of ailments and contagious diseases, and he will be much more responsive to your retraining efforts. For both man and canine, good health and aptitude go hand in hand.

And that brings us to the second most important person (after you) in your dog's life: his veterinarian. The choice of vet is up to you, of course, and it's necessarily limited if there's only one vet within fifty miles. Given a choice of vets, you'll waste time looking for a bargain, for their rates will be competitive—pretty much the same. If you're completely in the dark, check out the local vets with dog-owning friends and remember that all vets are not equal in experience, facilities, or reputation. We have always preferred a man or woman who attends to the needs of both large and small animals because of their broader experience.

The reality that many owners refuse to believe is that the average vet is not a fountain of knowledge when it comes to subjects not directly related to canine health and care. He or she is not the best-informed person around to ask about training, personality problems, breed temperament, show quality, or where the best pups of a given breed can be found. Vets are inundated with such non-veterinary questions every working day, and most have developed stock answers that help the spread of misinformation more than the education of owners.

Few vets are breeders, fewer know much about training, and the very few who rate as experts on certain breeds are usually easy to identify—they are also AKC breed judges. The simple truth is that most vets don't have the time for hobbies and special interests. They have enough trouble finding the hours to treat their animal patients and keeping up-to-date on the latest findings in the veterinary world. Find a good vet and you'll find yourself looking at an overworked man or woman. Put them all together—the good and the mediocre—and there are only about fifteen thousand small animal vets now practicing in the United States. Since there are many more pets than people in this country, it's reasonable to say that vets are in short supply.

There's no real relief in sight. In a good year, our veterinary schools—twenty here, three in Canada—graduate around sixteen hundred new vets. Most find immediate employment in industry, government, and research, but some five hundred do enter private practice. This is just about enough to replace vets who have retired, died, or gone to work for a zoo or a meat packer. So the real number of vets doctoring the needs of pets remains fairly constant, and the three more vet schools now in the planning stages won't help much. While it's possible that the combined schools will be graduating as many as two thousand new vets by 1990, the big majority won't go into private practice. If the dog and cat populations keep exploding, pet owners will be making appointments several weeks in advance. Who knows what will happen in emergencies?

If you have found a good vet, the statistics just enumerated should indicate how fortunate you are. Hold on to him or her, but don't expect either one to know why Sport won't drink pink lemonade and why he barks at three in the morning, or how to train him to swim underwater, or if he's too tall for a Puli. And if the good vet surprises you with answers that seem logical, don't blame me when they are proven otherwise.

I don't know how old you are, but when I was a boy, the family doctor thought nothing of making house calls, especially when children were sick. Many parents regarded their doctor as an authority on a wide range of subjects, such as the best trees to plant, the right colleges and professions for their children, when it would rain again, and should a President vote for his own reelection. People tend to believe healers. It must be a private law, and most healers—the old family doctor and today's vet—obey and proclaim.

The time to listen to a vet is when he's discussing the health of your dog. Other listening is at your own peril.

# Chapter 8

# WHAT DOGS DON'T KNOW ABOUT THEMSELVES

Heredity

The unhappiest dog lovers in America are the people who adopt or buy healthy-looking pets that are fated to become crippled or blind. An alarming number of dogs inherit HD (hip dysplasia) and/or PRA (progressive retinal atrophy), two of the commonest defects found in the canine world. While many unfortunate abnormalities are peculiar to just one or a few breeds, HD and PRA affect many breeds and are apparently here to stay.

HD is a misfit of the femur head (leg bone) and the hip socket. A mild case does not really impair a dog's mobility and cannot be visually detected, although the dog may prefer resting to running. In a severe case, the dog is in obvious pain whenever he changes positions and his hindquarters move in awkward fashion. Whenever somebody tells you that his dog is suffering from arthritis, it's fair to suspect that the dog has HD—unless x-rays prove otherwise.

While the abnormality pops up in all breeds, it is found most frequently in those with some size (over thirty pounds), particularly in the popular breeds, and especially in the German Shepherd dog. Only the breeders can control HD, and thus far not enough of them seem to care.

HD is never present at birth. It usually appears somewhere between a dog's fifth and twenty-fourth month of life, and even mild cases can be detected by radiograph. Over a period of time, HD can worsen, but it does not lessen and there is no cure, although new surgery has been developed to give at least temporary relief. No matter the degree of his defect, an HD dog should never be bred, since it is almost certain that he will pass along the structural weakness to some or all of his pups, and it has been proven that HD can also skip at least two generations.

While any breeder who can read must know that HD dogs should not be bred, the scientific proof is not a law, and 80 percent of our breeders don't even bother to test their dogs for HD. Of those that do, only a minority bother to go to the OFA (Orthopedic Foundation for Animals), the top HD authority in the land. The OFA experts read radiographs of dogs (two years and older) and issue clean-hip certificates for those dogs that qualify. Thus, an OFA-certified dog is considered safe for breeding. It would be safer if both its parents were OFA cleared, and much safer if all four grandparents were, too.

Some of the nicest people I know are breeders of dogs. Not just average or inexperienced breeders, but top breeders, famous from coast to coast and almost as well known as their dogs. All but one of them continues to breed dogs with mild cases of HD. They constantly remind me that the AKC has approved (in print). It's a strange world. The one breeder who doesn't is renowned for her Greyhounds, members of the only breed that has managed to escape HD. The breed is built differently from other over-thirty pounders and has a greater pelvic muscle mass to support the hips.

While most cases of HD develop after ten months, PRA

can come along as early as three months and as late as five years. The first symptom is always night blindness: the dog seems afraid of the outdoors at night, or of a dark room, and soon he has trouble with stairs and bumps into things, and his eyes turn a strange orange-green hue. PRA can only get progressively worse and result in blindness. Like HD, it is found in almost all breeds, although it is commoner in some breeds than others: Collie, Greyhound, Toy and Miniature Poodle, Miniature Dachshund, Norwegian Elkhound, and all setters, retrievers, and spaniels. And it is also passed down from either parent to pups.

Obviously, PRA dogs should not be bred, but many are. Compounding the problem is the fact that when a PRA pup shows up in a given litter, all the unaffected pups can be suspected of delaying the inevitable for another generation, since they are probably carriers of the causative gene. So that's another thing shared with HD: active PRA can and does skip a generation—too frequently.

Unlike HD, there's no major clearing house to certify a dog's freedom from PRA, but skilled veterinarians with the proper equipment (ophthalmoscope) can now offer a pretty good guarantee. That's something, if you are thinking of breeding, but it isn't everything. When you know that there's been PRA in your dog's family, the vet can't be absolutely sure that he's not a carrier. If you want to help in the fight against PRA, don't take the chance. Don't breed.

Since the average pet dog is acquired for the long term, it would seem that a dog lover versed in the dangers of HD and PRA could lessen the chance of heartbreak by selecting a breed classified as toy or miniature. But small dogs have hereditary problems, too, and the commonest is PD (patella dysplasia). This is a dislocation of the knee cap on one or both hind legs. Although corrections can be made, recurrence is sure and vet bills will mount. Again, PD dogs shouldn't be bred, but they are, and you're a real gambler if your Chihuahua, Maltese, Shih Tzu, Papillon, or Yorkshire Terrier came from a pet store. If some of the best breeders will take chances, you can imagine what the dingbats are using as breeding stock.

The canine has other hereditary defects—some found in all breeds, others in just one or two—and it would take a bigger book than this to list all of them. The awful truth is that the pet dog has many more physical defects than any other domestic animal, although he also has more breeds and varieties. The reasons for the abundance of abnormalities are many and people known as breeders must share the responsibility for not wiping them out. Still, in every breed, there are always those who have been very careful and dogs from their lines are not risky. Many of those worthy breeders are always active, but in the popular breeds, they are also greatly outnumbered by the dingbat breeders (see Chapter 1), so the percentage of quality, trouble-free dogs runs along at about 30 percent.

Since temperament is inherited, those dingbats are also responsible for most of the shy or vicious or stubborn or plain stupid dogs making life miserable for second owners, their families, and neighbors. So if your secondhand dog is a purebred troublemaker or difficult to retrain, the fault may not be his. As the dog said when he bit the hand that fed him, "Sorry, but I didn't ask to be whelped and I never met my mean sire."

The most active dingbats concentrate on the twenty most popular breeds, since pups of those breeds are the easiest to sell. Whether or not a second owner has a choice of breed, the risk is greatest when the dog belongs to the top twenty— unless one knows the breeder's rep or other members of the dog's family tree. Of course, it's always possible to check with the dog's vet or another breeder recommended by the vet. And for anyone who just can't wait to become the second owner of a particular breed, but nobody has offered a dog, contacting the nearest humane societies is always a good idea. They are great sources for older dogs of proven temperament.

On to the top twenty breeds, the ones to be wary about when accepting or selecting. As you study them, remember that a few represent the breed in all sizes and/or coats. These are the Poodle (Toy, Miniature, and Standard), the Beagle (13 inch and 15 inch), the Dachshund (Miniature and Standard, three coats), and the Collie (Rough and Smooth). Onward:

1) Poodle
2) Doberman Pinscher
3) German Shepherd
4) Cocker Spaniel
5) Irish Setter
6) Labrador Retriever
7) Beagle
8) Dachshund
9) Miniature Schnauzer
10) Golden Retriever
11) Shetland Sheepdog
12) Collie
13) Lhasa Apso
14) Yorkshire Terrier
15) Siberian Husky
16) Pekingese
17) Brittany Spaniel
18) English Springer Spaniel
19) Great Dane
20) Pomeranian

The Poodle has been top dog since 1960, when he replaced the Beagle, who had toppled the Cocker Spaniel back in 1953. The chance of any other pure breed replacing the Poodle during the next decade is extremely remote. Obviously, this breed has a lot going for it. In any size or color, the average Poodle possesses a high canine IQ, and both the good ones and the bad ones wear a nonshedding coat. The coat has made the breed the favorite of fastidious housekeepers and people who are usually allergic to dogs. Most allergy-prone dog lovers can also find happiness with the

Bedlington Terrier, Kerry Blue Terrier (if you like your dogs rough, tough, and lots of fun), and Portuguese Water dog.

## HE OR SHE

There has never been a law against holding fast to preconceived notions and that's why the battle of the canine sexes may never end. All other things being equal, which sex makes the better pet?

What you are about to read is based on experience with numerous dogs of each sex in several breeds, plus the experiences of many friends in other breeds. The consensus of opinions relates only to housedogs, since those are the ones we observe the most and know the best, several at a time. Ladies first.

*Bitches, pro:* pups develop faster in both IQ and body. At any age, they are more adaptable and easier to train. Adults usually achieve less size than their litter brothers and mix well with other bitches and males. And as canines go, are more apt to respect the social niceties imposed by people.

*And con:* they are tricky and less trustworthy and thus rather independent. The big complaint of most people concerns the heat periods. Spaying is the answer, and for those who object to that, the alternative solution is the prescription medication that delays the heat period for any amount of time.

*Males, pro:* more anxious to please, less curious than their sisters, and thus less apt to test an owner's wits.

*And con:* not much of a mixer in a canine crowd, in that he prefers the company of the opposite sex. More destructive (often accidentally) around the house, and more apt to roam—especially when a bitch in heat lives within three miles. And traditionally, a male pup costs more. Also eats more.

As for neutering (either sex), it really doesn't change a

dog's personality or noble qualities, nor does it correct bad and offensive habits. The chief benefit to mankind is that the neutered dog cannot reproduce, thus reducing the future canine population by an infinitesimal amount. Aside from being rendered impossible for breeding, the only drawback for a purebred is that he or she becomes ineligible for appearances in the breed ring and a try for the title of show champion. Whether pure or mixed breed, a castrated Romeo isn't like to be shot by the irate owner of a bitch in season, and a spayed Dinah Loverly won't deposit unwanted pups on your doorstep. And in most communities, the cost for a neutered dog's license is reduced.

Some very popular myths to the contrary, spaying or castrating does not make a dog fat or listless or more agreeable. And the surgery does not shorten longevity. Indeed, a strong case could be made for the belief that neutering prolongs life. Altered canines do seem to live to a ripe old age. Spaying does control a host of female problems, and castration is often the cure for certain skin and coat problems and certainly cuts down on marking.

Most vets agree that the wrong time to spay a bitch is during her heat cycle. They differ as to the earliest age: quite young (three months), prior to first heat period (about one year in most breeds). The local vote is for the latter choice, since it gives the bitch more time for overall development. At the other end of the life scale, the surgery can be safely performed at any time (between heat cycles), and breeders usually spay brood bitches after their last litters, at seven or eight years. Males are castrated after their first birthday and up to their sixth.

OF TEMPERATURE AND AGE

The truest indicator of a dog's health is his temperature. For most dogs, it's 101.2 degrees F. although it does vary a bit for some individuals, and might be a tenth or so off depending on the time of day (lower in the AM, higher in the PM). You won't get a true reading if the dog has been running or playing. He should relax for about twenty minutes.

Have the dog standing and use a rectal thermometer. Lightly coat this with Vaseline and insert (more than an inch) with a gentle, twisting motion. Remove after three minutes, clean with tissue, and read. If the dog is a full degree off the 101.2 mark, something is wrong. If more than a degree off, it's time to call the vet.

If somebody in your family becomes ill, you probably take his or her temperature before calling the doctor, since that's one of the first things the medical expert wants to know. The same goes for the vet.

Dogs don't know that, of course, but every owner should —and the majority don't. Another thing that every dog doesn't know or care about is his age. He has two ages: real and equivalent.

The one that matters is his *real* age and it is measured at the rate of twelve months per year, even as yours and mine. His longevity is figured at twelve to fourteen years (double the 1900 figure), although that's a medial estimate. The giant breeds never achieve it and the small ones often surpass it. The oldest dog ever (on record) was a Labrador Retriever who lived beyond the age of twenty-seven (1936-1963, England). That's twice the average Lab's span.

A dog's *equivalent* age is only important to owners who wonder how old Bert the Bloodhound would be if he were a man. The comparative-age scales have changed many times since people first started wondering about equivalent ages, but the thinking has been firm for the last couple of decades and today an authority on the subject will tell you this:

At the age of one, Bert would be fifteen—if he were a boy. At two, Bert would be twenty-four—if he were a man.

Thereafter, every canine year is the equivalent of four mortal years. Thus, when Bert is equivalently ninety-six, he will really be only twenty—although that's old enough to set a new, world longevity record for Bloodhounds.

## CHANGING NAMES

Some people really dislike certain names, and that's why my boyhood friend Archibald S. King is now known as A. Samuel King. About a year ago, friend Sam phoned and asked me to find a chocolate Labrador pup for his grandson Bob, age twelve. I told Sam that he was in luck, as I knew somebody who wanted to place his chocolate Lab in a good home and I could recommend the dog. Sam was delighted, but not Bob. The boy wouldn't even look at the dog because his name was Percival.

We could not convince Bob that it would be easy to change the dog's name. "He's over a year and that's too old for him to learn a new name," was the boy's argument. I don't know where he got that information, but he should return it. The girl who eventually became Percival's second owner did not like his name either, so she changed it to Bobby. Took less than a week.

If you want to change your dog's name, do it. He won't mind, and he's never too old to learn something as simple as a new term of endearment. The changeover will occur more rapidly if you and everyone who address the dog use his new name and completely forget his old one. During the first few days, make a point of overdoing the use of the new name whenever you and the dog are one-on-one, or when you're petting, praising, grooming, and feeding him.

Should you take advantage of your legal and moral rights as a second owner, you'll help yourself, your dog and your cause by selecting a pet or call name that meets these two standards:

1. It should be quite short. This is a convenience for the owner, especially when he must shout it into the wind. At the same time, the dog recognizes his name (really the sound of it) in more of a hurry, and this speeds up the training process.

2. It should have a distinct sound of its own. All this means is that the name should not sound like a command word or a correction. Training is impeded when similar sounds cause confusion. If you follow this sound advice, you will not name your dog Noel (no), Syd (sit), Rum (come), Kenneth (kennel), Dom or Don (down), Ray or Clay (stay), and Neil (heel).

This illustrates why some dog fanciers are apt to invent strange call names for their dogs. A switch in names may confuse the dogs a bit, but only for a few days. The canine can relate to a new name (sound) in a hurry, provided he no longer hears the old name (sound).

And in the long run—as when dog and master have achieved a mysterious understanding of each other—the dog is capable of responding to several names. That's always been the case in my home. For reasons that nobody has ever explained, this writer seldom forgets a face—human or animal—but has a spotty record with names. So Skipper responds to numerous names, and so do all of our other dogs. Out of necessity, they have learned it is the only way to live in harmony with me. So it is possible for me to report that once a dog has mastered his given name and reached maturity, he is capable of learning other names. Not by the dozen, but at least four or five. Somehow, once you and your dog get to know each other very well, he seems to sense that he's the one you're addressing—even when you use another name.

Visitors are sometimes confused when they ask to see my dog Skipper and I call out for Jody or Jimmy and Skipper

*He won't care what you call him as long as you call him.*

arrives. They are always confused when they visit the kennel of my friend Joyce Pelham, who breaks with tradition by being contrariwise in the naming process. "And this is Harry, the dam of the pups you just saw," Joyce will explain. "Please come this way and I'll show you Peggy, their sire."

Joyce's other brood bitches are George and Richard, and she also owns Peggy's brother, Sally. All five are happy Giant Schnauzers and the names do not seem to embarrass them. They are living proof that any name is appropriate in an environment of TLC.

Given a choice, most second owners prefer young dogs, the ones that haven't lived long enough to pick up a repertory of bad habits. But more than a million dog lovers per annum don't have that choice. For better or worse, they become owners of dogs inherited from dearly beloved and often late lamented relatives, and the tail waggers are frequently elderly. They do require extra consideration and care, and most of them certainly deserve the added attention. They were devoted, affectionate companions. They brought joy to their first owners, they are capable of doing it again, and—as with people—some are not nearly as old as they look. It's not that the dogs have worried too much. Rather, they've eaten too much and they are overweight, an unhealthy state for both beast and man.

Granted that he gets sufficient exercise, a dog will stay in great shape for years on the same daily ration. The quantity remains the same all through his prime, and it's less than when he was a young adult and far less than he required as a pup. The efficiency of his digestive system has improved over the years, and it continues to improve past his prime and into old age. Now he's slowing down and burning less energy, and also extracting more calories from his food. The excess is transformed into fat, then eventual obesity and its related problems. All this on the same daily ration that has kept the dog in the pink of condition for years and years.

The cure for overweight is the reduction in quantity of the daily ration. Age does not dim appetite, so the dog is bound to be unhappy as he slims to respectable proportions. Fat does not come off in a hurry and should not be encouraged to do so. Thus, shave a little of the ration each week, and don't be surprised if there's no weight change for a couple of weeks. To avoid serious side effects, a dog the size of a Collie should lose no more than eight ounces per week. To avoid his complaints, adding cooked vegetables to the shrinking dinners will fool his eyes, fill his tummy, and leave him content. Summer or winter squash, turnip, old lettuce, spinach, carrot, and beet are fine, but avoid members of the cabbage family. And to avoid a personal feeling of guilt, adding a touch of high protein (boiled egg, cooked fish) won't add weight. The fats and carbohydrates (grains) are the problems.

Overweight dog lovers tend to raise overweight dogs, and that's even true of obese dog fanciers who should know better—and do, when it counts. You don't see fat dogs in Obedience, where extra pounds would hinder performance, and you don't often see them in the breed ring, where the very look of fitness counts. But if you go to the kennels of those too heavy fanciers and look at their other dogs, the ones who aren't competing in public or being readied, you'll see round old-timers and potbellied pups.

Shrinking the daily ration week by week is the simplest way to take poundage off the old dog. All during this rather long process, he is also living off some of his stored energy, in that he's burning off his excess fat. The same results can be achieved through exercise and without reducing the daily ration. This second-best method calls for a plentiful daily exercise until the right weight is reached, and then sufficient daily exercise forevermore to keep the dog at that weight. Since old dogs seldom exercise for long without encouragement, the method is both time consuming and fatiguing for owners who are not professional athletes.

The third method is expensive. There are several excellent diet foods on the market that are designed for canine reducing programs. Each is a prescription food and is only available from a vet. The foods do satisfy the canine's appe-

tite and provide him with all the nutrition he needs. They are safe to feed and they do get results, and many people think they represent the kindest way to take weight off an old dog or an extremely obese dog of any age. They are certainly an easy way.

*135*

Well, overweight isn't the only problem old dogs have, but it's the commonest and not really their fault. An old dog in the pink is a step slower than last year. If he's also fat, he's several steps slower—and not aware of that fact. So if he still chases cars, the sport is now extremely dangerous and he must be trained to desist or be fenced. He is neither too slow nor too lazy for training, of course.

There is absolutely no indication that a dog knows or senses that he has lived long enough to be considered (by people) a senior citizen of the canine world. He can't run as far or as fast or as long as he did in his heyday, but he'll give it his best shot—short bursts and rests in between—and eventually reach his goal. And if he's an outdoor dog and wears a long coat, he now feels the cold of winter nights that he once took in stride. The coat of old age is under par in thickness, suppleness, and sheen.

What all this boils down to is the fact that the old dog needs more of everything except food. He needs more attention and care, more rest and less strenuous play, and always more warmth than cold. The lucky old dog also enjoys more supervised travel, in terms of visits to the vet. Some of the visits may prove unnecessary, but the owner will find peace of mind and everybody but the dog will know that he really cares.

The few dogs who manage to reach old age without coming close to a vet help to perpetuate the rumor that aging builds immunity to canine diseases. Believers who skip the annual booster shots (see Chapter 1) do save money, but only in the short run. Left unprotected, old dogs are sure candidates for distemper and—if they socialize with other dogs or share the grounds they visited—likely victims of hepatitis or leptospirosis. The money saved becomes dogs lost forever.

Still, even those who do get the shots are not really home free. The chances of eye, ear, and skin problems are greater as the aging process continues, and allergies and hormonal deficiencies often come into play. The trick is to catch and treat them early, and that's why any vet worthy of a good reputation gives an old dog more than a cursory examination whenever the pet is on hand for a shot.

We always have two or three old-timers underfoot, and suspicion is the main reason why they stay healthy and happy for so long. They don't do the suspecting. We do. Whenever an old dog shows signs of distress, it's time to suspect the worst and hop on the phone to the vet. Waiting around for the dog to repeat the performance might cost his life. When old age comes to a dog, his most serious problems don't develop gradually. They erupt, and the dog needs immediate help.

Kidney trouble is common. The old dog's kidneys are functioning at less than half their former efficiency and the chances of something going wrong are enhanced. Violent vomiting, severe diarrhea, excessive drinking of water, constant urinating, bad breath, staggering and fainting are all signs of some type of kidney disease. Caught in time and treated, recovery is usual.

Old dogs are less likely to have heart trouble than people, and more likely to enjoy complete recovery from strokes. Cataracts, conjunctivitis, loss of hearing, anemia, skin trouble, true arthritis, and problems with internal and external parasites become more likely in canine old age. And then there is cancer. It need not be fatal. Some cases can be cured, and in others the spread can be slowed or contained. While cancer does kill thousands of old dogs every year, as many as half die needlessly—because the malady wasn't detected in time. The old dog really should be checked by the vet every six months rather than annually. It does give him a better shot at a longer life. That's every six months for ALL dogs that reach the age of ten. Including the few giant dogs that reach that age, although they should have been on that schedule since they were five years old.

Even when eligible, the purebred old-timer is over the hill insofar as the breed ring goes and he doesn't have any chance of picking up all the points he needs for a show champion title. It's not that he can't handle the simple routine, but that much younger and flashier and better-coated dogs always catch the judge's eyes. Happily, Obedience is a different story and it's never too late for a dog to begin—so long as he meets the AKC qualifications (Chapter 7) and can still trot.

Any qualifier can be trained to earn his CD degree, and the CDX is available for the old dog that can still take the high jump. For most breeds, the jump is half again the dog's height at the withers (i.e., thirty inches for a twenty-inch dog), and for a few, the jump is set at precisely the same height as the dog's. Most of those few breeds are the ones nature did not design for jumping: all the longish terriers, plus the Basset Hound, Bulldog, French Bulldog, Dachshund, Welsh Corgi, Maltese, Pekingese, Clumber and Sussex Spaniels. And these breeds also jump their own height, but never more than thirty-six inches: Bloodhound, Bullmastiff, Great Dane, Great Pyrenees, Mastiff, Newfoundland, and St. Bernard.

A few old dogs do go on to earn the UD every year. Each is an exception and something of a miracle, too. Speed, vision, and hearing haven't diminished much, and the same can be said for the dog's sense of smell. You can bet that the dog's owner has done most things right, year after year after year.

*Seniors together*

To have a real shot at success in Obedience, the old dog must be in the best possible shape. He cannot reach the goal without the cooperation of his owner, who must provide the right diet, opportunity for exercise, and a training program. All this keeps the dog from becoming fat and listless, and the owner from complaining. It is a healthy endeavor for both.

I enjoy watching old dogs go through their paces at

Obedience trials. They seem to take more pride in their performances than the young adults, while ignoring distractions and accepting applause as just one of those things. When a junior breaks on a long sit or down, the old dog regards him with tolerance. And he's amused when his high score causes his owner's ego to shine brightly. I can almost hear the dog's thoughts: "Will you look at that two-legged, tailless ninny? You'd think *he* won the ribbon, the cash, and all the trophies."

The oldest dog we ever started in Obedience was Folly. She was a little over twelve when she entered her first trial and scored a qualifying 194 under a very tough judge. Normally, that might not be cause for a celebration, but Folly's case was rather unusual, for she had not had any real training for Obedience. On the other hand, she had plenty of experience watching other Labs of ours being trained, and Evie often used her as a post (figure eight) or as company (long sits and downs). So while Folly was Obedience untrained, she was a trained observer. She went to that first trial without a single minute of practice with my wife, who would handle her, or anyone else.

I was there and I watched their teamwork with hope and many reservations. When it was over, friendly dog fanciers and spectators crowded about Evie and offered their congratulations. I was standing alone, holding Folly's trophies and a bit disappointed that she hadn't won a small halo. The judge approached and asked, "The yellow Lab bitch is yours?"

"My wife's."

"Oh, yes. I just learned the bitch is over twelve. A very impressive performance! I hope you campaign her."

"I'll deliver the message."

"Please do. Well, your face is familiar and I know you write about dogs, but I just can't remember names."

"I'm Senator Baxter Westminster."

"Oh, you're in politics, too?"

"It's my hobby."

"Well, I hope you find the time to write about the old dog in Obedience some day. The subject belongs in a book, really. There's no reason for senior dogs to be inactive. Or senior people, for that matter. Good-bye, Senator."

We shook hands and parted. I wish I could remember the judge's name. I'd send him a copy of this book.

# INDEX

*142*